QTS LITERACY TUTOR

Pass your

Literacy Skills Test

David Chryssides

ISBN-13: 9781793371201

CONTENTS

QTS LITERACY TUTOR
WWW.LITERACYSKILLSTEST.CO.UK

FREE ONLINE LITERACY SKILLS TEST
EXPERT 1 TO 1 TUITION WITH OUR QTS SPECIALISTS

--- **WHAT QTS LITERACY TUTOR HAS TO OFFER** ---

| Spelling Practice | Punctuation Questions | Grammar Section | Comprehension Resources |

| Practice Tests | Expert Tutors | Correct Format | New Question Formats |

Visit www.literacyskillstest.co.uk to take a Free Full Practice Test today.

10
LITERACY SKILLS TESTS

97%
LEARNER PASS RATE

490
TEST QUESTIONS

QTS MATHS TUTOR
WWW.QTSMATHSTUTOR.CO.UK

FREE ONLINE NUMERACY SKILLS TEST
EXPERT 1 TO 1 TUITION WITH OUR QTS SPECIALISTS

--- **WHAT QTS MATHS TUTOR HAS TO OFFER** ---

21 Numeracy Skills Tests

12 Topic Revision Tests

Over 120 Video Solutions

Regularly Updated Questions

Expert 1 to 1 Tuition Service

Written Solutions to every question

Visit www.qtsmathstutor.co.uk to take a **Free Full Practice Test today.**

21
NUMERACY SKILLS TESTS

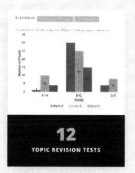
12
TOPIC REVISION TESTS

650+
MODEL SOLUTIONS

1.0   Introduction

First of all, congratulations on purchasing this book. You now have the key to passing the QTS literacy skills test!

This is a book to help you pass the test, and not a book on how to master the intricacies of the English language. This book will not teach you how to use a colon or semicolon correctly in your writing, but it will tell you how to add a colon or semicolon in a poorly punctuated piece of text, since this is what you need to do in the test itself.   This also means that I have tried to avoid using technical jargon where possible, so I have tried to steer clear of terms that might confuse rather than assist.

If you have already experienced some of the questions that appear in the QTS numeracy test, you have no doubt said to yourself, "Why on earth do I need to know this to become a teacher?" When the person in question wants to be, say, a secondary drama teacher, it does seem a little bit unnecessary to have to learn how to interpret a box and whisker plot, since it is not going to make any difference to a drama teacher's ability to do his or her job effectively. However, when it comes to literacy, I feel much more strongly about the legitimacy of this test since, whatever subject you are planning to teach, whether it be in a primary or secondary school, you cannot escape the need for having a strong command of the English language. Teachers need to be ambassadors for the English language, ensuring that the children in their care end up with a good command of the English language, rather than pick up a teacher's sloppy errors.

As well as requiring good literacy skills to help the students you teach, remember that your literacy skills may be judged in every email you send to fellow members of staff, or letters sent to parents concerning a school trip you are organising, and if your communications are riddled with basic English errors then, firstly, this is not very professional and, secondly, fellow members of staff, and especially certain parents, will leap to conclusions about your ability to teach.

We have to accept that we all make mistakes with the English language from time to time. No one is perfect! However, we can all make improvements in our literacy, whether it is in spelling or in the correct use of punctuation or grammar, and that perhaps we could use the QTS literacy skills test as an opportunity to move our literacy skills up a level, rather than seeing this test as another random hoop to jump through. Remember that whatever subject we teach, literacy is crucial, and we need to model correct use of the English language for the sake of our students.

1.1   About the test

The QTS literacy test is divided into four sections: spelling, punctuation, grammar and reading comprehension. Unless you have special arrangements, you have 45 minutes to complete the test. The total number of marks available in the test is between 45 and 49 and is broken down as follows:

Spelling – 10 marks

Punctuation – 15 marks

Grammar – 10 – 12 marks

Reading Comprehension - 10 – 12 marks

8

The pass mark of the test does vary slightly according to the difficulty of the test, but is normally set around the 65% mark.

The spelling section is the only part of the test which you cannot revisit once you have submitted your answers. You are able to review your answers in the other three sections, meaning that if you are struggling with a given question, you can flag it, move on, and come back to it later, time permitting of course.

1.2   About this book

This book follows the same sequence as the test itself, so it is divided into four chapters. You do not need to read the four chapters in order; they are all stand-alone, and some can be completely omitted if you do not have any difficulties in that area. In the punctuation chapter, there are some practice questions for you to attempt to prove mastery of a particular punctuation point. Following the four chapters of explanations, there are three mock tests which also include answers as well as some explanations as to why answers are correct or incorrect.

2.0   Spelling

- Questions: 10
- Marks: 10
- Percentage of paper: 20% - 22%
- Recommended time spent on this paper: 5 minutes
- What is considered a good mark for this section? 8 or above

The spelling section has to be completed first, and is the only part of the test that cannot be revisited once you have finished it. The reason for this is that the word you have been asked to spell could appear in a text later in the test, therefore giving the answer away.

In this section of the test, you have ten sentences, each with one word missing. You have to listen to the missing word by clicking on an audio icon, and then have to type this missing word in the box provided. You are able to listen to the word as many times as you like, and I would recommend listening to it numerous times just to check that you are certain of the word you are being asked to spell.

There is also a non-audio version of the test where you have to select the correct spelling of the word from a list (similar to the spelling questions in the mock tests in this book). If you are eligible for the non-audio version, then make sure that you have made special arrangements for this in advance.

I have heard people say that they are 'naturally bad spellers'. Unless you are dyslexic, then you are not naturally bad at spelling. It is more likely that your school or college neglected to point out your errors of usage, or failed to teach them. Do not allow yourself to have a fixed mind-set on this and believe that, with a bit of practice, you can make improvements on your spelling!

With a bit of work on the spellings of the more difficult words (since these are the words that you are more likely to be tested on), and applying some of the general rules that I have included below, you should be looking to tackle this part of the test with confidence, and achieving full marks is certainly a possibility. Remember too that the DfE (Department for Education) does not provide a list of words to test you on; however, the words that you are going to be tested on are likely to be words which you might use in your professional role, words which you would conceivably use if you were writing to a parent or colleague, or writing an end of year report for a student (so the word 'cemetery' is probably not a word to be too concerned about, whereas a word like 'differentiation' might be). On the QTS Literacy Tutor website, there is a list of recommended words to study for the spelling section. Google 'QTS Literacy Tutor Spelling' and you will find the spellings on the website.

Here are some general spelling 'rules', but remember that there are frequent exceptions to these rules.

2.1   Spelling tip 1: 'i' before 'e', except after 'c'

If people only remember one spelling rule, then it is this one. If you don't know this rule, remember that if a word has the letters 'i' and 'e' together, then the letter 'i' comes before the letter 'e', except when following the letter 'c'.

believe ('i' before 'e')

piece ('i' before 'e')

conceit ('i' before 'e', except after 'c')

receipt ('i' before 'e', except after 'c')

However, this rule only applies when the sound is an 'ee' sound. When the 'i' and the 'e' come together and do not make an 'ee' sound, then the 'i' comes after the 'e'

beige ('i' after the 'e' because the sound is not 'ee')

neighbour ('i' after the 'e' because the sound is not 'ee')

There are exceptions to this rule, like the word 'caffeine'. While the substance itself may be very useful in the teaching profession, it is unlikely to be a word you need to write all that often as a teacher, so therefore highly unlikely to appear in the test.

2.2   Spelling tip 2: 'y' becomes an 'i'

When a word ends with the letter 'y' in the singular form, the 'y' changes to an '-ies' in the plural:

body – bodies

lady – ladies

supply – supplies

difficulty - difficulties

However, this rule does not apply to words that end in a vowel and a letter 'y':

one day – two days

one way – many ways

This 'y' becoming an 'i' rule also affects verb forms too:

I try – he tries

we fly – she flies

It also affects suffixes (endings):

apply – application

fancy - fanciful

2.3   Spelling tip 3: dropping the letter 'e'

If you are adding a suffix (e.g. '-ing', '-able', '-ible', '-ion', '-tion', '-ous') to a word which ends with the letter 'e' and the suffix begins with a vowel, then you drop the 'e'.

hope – hoping

adore - adorable

procrastinate – procrastination

relate – relation

However, the letter 'e' is not dropped when the word ends in '-ce' or '-ge'. If the letter 'e' were dropped, then the word would be pronounced with a hard 'c' or 'g', which would be wrong:

advantage – advantageous

peace - peaceable

2.4   Spelling tip 4: consonant doubling rule

This rule helps explain why some words have a double consonant when a suffix is added, and why others do not:

stop – stopped (doubling)

work – worked (no doubling)

In a word with one syllable, you need to double the final consonant if the word ends in one vowel and one consonant:

chat – chatting

cram – cramming

grip - gripping

In a word with more than one syllable, double the final consonant if the word ends in a vowel and a consonant, and the final syllable is stressed:

beGIN – beginning (consonant doubled because final syllable is stressed)

preFER – preferring (consonant doubled because final syllable is stressed)

BENefit – benefited (consonant not doubled because final syllable is not stressed)

Note that the consonants 'w', 'x' and 'y' are never doubled.

However, for words that end in the letter 'l', you do double the 'l' even if the stress does not fall on the last syllable.

cancel – cancellation

model – modelling

enrol – enrolling (however the word 'enrolment' only has one 'l' because this rule of doubling the letter 'l' only applies when you are adding a suffix beginning with a vowel)

2.5   Spelling tip 5: adding '-ful'

Do not confuse the spelling of the word 'full' (not empty) which has a double 'l' with the suffix '-ful' which always has a single 'l':

doubt**ful**

colour**ful**

peace**ful**

However, the suffix '-fully' has a double 'l':

hope**fully**

peace**fully**

2.6   Spelling tip 6: adding prefixes

It is highly likely that you will be asked to spell at least one word which contains a prefix. A prefix is added to the beginning of a word to amend its meaning, often to make the word have the opposite meaning.

happy – **un**happy

There are lots of different prefixes, the most common being: 'un', 'il', 'im', 'ir', 'mis' and 'dis'.

Do be careful with the prefix 'mis', which has a single letter 's' and not a double (think of the word 'mistake' which has one 's' and not two).

The key thing to remember is that when you add a prefix to a word, you may end up with a double letter. There is no need to drop a consonant. Note how the following words have a doubling of the consonant when the final letter of the prefix and the first letter of the root word are the same:

necessary – un**n**ecessary (un + necessary)

satisfied – di**ss**atisfied (dis + satisfied)

legal – i**ll**egal (il + legal)

relevant – i**rr**elevant (ir + relevant)

legible – i**ll**egible (il + legible)

Words like 'unnecessary' and 'dissatisfied' are often misspelled (as is the word 'misspelled' by the way!) and could feature in the spelling section of the test, so remember that it is a double and not a single consonant when you attach the prefix.

2.7 Spelling tip 7: sound it out!

Try breaking down words in your head to help you decode the spelling. A word like 'meticulous' can be problematic to spell, but if you say it to yourself, slowly, syllable by syllable, hopefully you will imagine the word as:

me / ti / cu / lous

However, this example does also have a complicated '-ous' ending which can be easy to get wrong.

16

complimentary – com / pli / men / ta / ry (remembering that it is an '-ary', not '-ery' ending)

implementation – im / ple / men / ta / tion (remembering that a '-tion' ending is used for the sound is 'shun')

detrimental – de / tri / men / tal (remembering that the ending is '-tal', not '-tel' or '-tle')

subsequently – sub / se / quent / ly (remembering that it is a '-que' not a '-cue')

particularly – par / ti / cu / lar / ly (remembering that it is '-lar-' and not '-ler-')

administrative – ad / min / i / stra / tive

capabilities – ca / pa / bil / i / ties (remembering that when a noun ending in 'y' in the singular changes to an '-ies' in the plural)

Breaking the words down to individual syllables can be a helpful technique but, as you can see from several of the examples above, it is still not a guarantee that the spelling is obvious!

2.8   Spelling tip 8: words with double consonants

Words which have a doubling of a consonant can be very challenging to spell, particularly if there are multiple consonant doublings, as there are no set rules. The words 'agree' and 'aggressive' have the same 'ag' sound for the first syllable, but there is one 'g' in 'agree', but two in 'aggressive'. The most common double letter combinations are 'll' (e.g. parallel), 'ss' (e.g.

possession), 'ee' (e.g. attend**ee**), 'oo' (e.g. c**oo**perate), 'ff' (e.g. di**ff**erentiation), 'pp' (e.g. o**pp**ortunity), 'rr' (e.g. i**rr**egular), 'mm' (e.g. com**m**unication).

Many words have a double consonant due to the addition of prefixes and suffixes (as described in earlier tips).

Remember that all words ending in '-ally' have a double 'l'.

Here is a list of problematic words. They are problematic because they have double consonant combinations, or because people think they should when they don't!

challenge	collaboration	syllable
intelligence	miscellaneous	colloquial
embarrassing	happening	millennium
occurrence	questionnaire	successful
difference	profession	accomplishment
personnel	recommend	fulfil
unnecessary	occasionally	occurred

2.9   Spelling tip 9: words that end in '-ance' and '-ence'

Words with these endings are often misspelled because these words endings sound the same when spoken. One way of working out the correct ending is to think of the verb that forms the basis of the '-ance' or '-ence' word.

If the verb ends in '-y', '-ure', '-ate' or '-ear', then the '-ance' ending is used:

comply – compli**ance**

endure – endur**ance**

18

tolerate - toler**ance**

appear – appear**ance**

If the ending follows a hard 'c' or 'g', then '-ance' is used:

signific**ance**

eleg**ance**

If the verb ends in '-ere', then the ending will be '-ence':

adhere – adher**ence**

interfere – interfer**ence**

If the final syllable of a verb that ends in '-er' is stressed, then the ending is '-ence':

refer – refer**ence**

confer – confer**ence**

If the word ends with an '-ide', then use '-ence':

confide - confid**ence**

reside - resid**ence**

If the word ends with a soft 'c' or 'g', then use '-ence':

intellig**ence**

innoc**ence**

If these words were spelt with the '-ance' ending, then the letters 'c' or 'g' would be pronounced with a hard sound, which would be wrong.

2.10   Spelling tip 10: words that end in '-ant' and '-ent'

These endings behave in a similar way to the rules for '-ance' and 'ence'.

If the verb ends in '-y', '-ure', '-ate' or '-ear', then the '-ant' ending is used:

comply – compli**ant**

tolerate – toler**ant**

If the ending follows a hard 'c' or 'g', then '-ant' is used:

signific**ant**

eleg**ant**

If the ending follows a soft 'c' or 'g', then '-ent' is used:

dec**ent**

intellig**ent**

dilig**ent**

If the ending follows an '-er' then '-ent' is used:

inher**ent**

coher**ent**

If the word ends with an '-id', then use '-ent':

confide - confid**ent**

reside - resid**ent**

2.11   Spelling tip 11: words that end in '-able' and '-ible'

An easy way to find out whether a word should be spelled with the '-able' or '-ible' ending is to remove this ending. Once you have removed the '-able' or '-ible' ending, are you left with an English word? If you are, then it should be '-able'. If not, it should be '-ible'.

breakable – take off the '-able' or '-ible', and you are left with the word 'break'. Since 'break' is a word in its own right, we must use the '-able' suffix.

acceptable – take off the '-able' or '-ible', and you are left with the word 'accept'. Since 'accept' is a word in its own right, we must use use the '-able' suffix.

visible – take off the '-able' or '-ible', and you are left with the word 'vis'. Since 'vis' is not a word in its own right, we must use the '-ible' suffix.

If you remove the suffix and you are left with a non-word that ends with a hard 'c' or 'g', then the suffix is '-able':

amicable (despite the fact that 'amic' is not a word in its own right)

2.12   Spelling tip 12:   words that end in '-ary', '-ery' and '-ory'

Most words that take the '-ery' suffix are related to words that end in '-er':

miser – mis**ery**

discover – discov**ery**

archer – arch**ery**

If you take the suffix off and you are left with a recognisable English word, then usually '-ery' is the correct suffix:

rob – robbery

forge – forgery

scene – scenery

If there is a similar word that ends in '-ion', then you should use the suffix '-ory':

introduction – introductory

explanation – explanatory

conservation – conservatory

If you remove the suffix and the word is not recognisable, then use the suffix '-ary'

vocabulary ('vocabul' is not a word)

necessary ('necess' is not a word)

Note that there are exceptions to these rules!

For spelling tips 9 – 12, there are a lot of rules to memorise so, rather than trying to memorise them all, perhaps a better strategy would be to learn how to spell a selection of the examples I have provided which you can apply to the words which may appear in the test.

2.13 Spelling tip 13: mnemonics and tricks

For those particularly challenging words, it may be worth thinking of mnemonics or other tricks to ensure that you can remember the spellings.

'Rhythm' is a really treacherous word, and a music teacher from my previous school taught the students the following mnemonic:

Rhythm Helps Your Two Hips Move

'Stationery', in the school equipment sense, was always a word I could never spell, as I mixed it up with the word 'stationary', meaning 'not moving'. To help me remember that it was '-ery' and not '-ary', I thought up a little trick: knowing that a pencil is a piece of school equipment, and that there is an 'e', but no 'a' in 'pencil', this helped me to remember that it was 'stationery' with an 'e' and not 'stationary' with an 'a'. It really doesn't matter how pathetic the trick you make up is, and if it's one that you think of yourself, then it should be easier to remember. With a bit of imagination you should be able to think of something to help you spell any of those words that you find particularly difficult.

2.14 Tips for spelling practice

1. Get someone to test you. Give someone (perhaps someone who is in the same situation as you so you feel less awkward / embarrassed) a list of words that you are trying to spell correctly. Get them to read a word to you and you spell it back. Make sure that the person testing you really focuses on your weaknesses; if you have spelled a word incorrectly, expect to be tested on this word repeatedly until you have mastered it.

2. Use a voice recorder. Record a list of words on your mobile phone. Play the list back to yourself, pausing after every word. Write the word down, and then compare to your original word list.

3. Look, say, hide, write, check. Take a quick look at the word, say it to yourself a few times, then write it and compare with the correct spelling. This is less effective than previous options since, by having a quick glance at the correct spelling of the word, you have cheated a little bit. However, every time you write a word accurately, you are embedding its correct spelling in your brain.

4. Flashcards. Write a sentence on the front of the flashcard which contains the word you are learning to spell, but leave a gap for the word that you are practising. Write down the missing word on a separate piece of paper and check with the reverse of the flashcard to see if the spelling is accurate. For example:

    the boy's b.......... is starting to improve (front of flashcard)
    behaviour (back of flashcard)

5. Use the practice tests on QTS Literacy Tutor along with the practice papers on the DfE website to give you plenty of practise in the real exam format.

3.0   Punctuation

- Questions: 1
- Marks: 15
- Percentage of paper: 30% - 33%
- Recommended time spent on this paper: 10 minutes
- What is considered a good mark for this section? 12 or above

The punctuation section of the test has the largest allocation of marks, so it is crucial to ensure that your revision for the test focuses on this. With a bit of practice, this should be a quick and easy way to score as close to full marks as possible.

In the punctuation section of the test, you are required to insert 15 punctuation omissions from a text. This does not necessarily mean that you have to insert 15 punctuation *marks* (missing commas, speech marks, question marks, colons etc.); a punctuation omission can also include the capitalisation of a lower case word and the creation of a new paragraph.

Below is a list of the 12 punctuation options you will have, followed later by explanations and examples of how to use them correctly in practice questions.

- a full stop .
- a comma ,
- a question mark ?
- a colon :
- a semi-colon ;
- a speech mark (a double quotation mark) "

- an inverted comma (a single quotation mark) '
- an apostrophe (identical symbol to the inverted comma above) '
- a bracket (or)
- a hyphen -
- capitalisation of a word
- new paragraph //

Sometimes in the text, you may see two omissions together. If there is a missing full stop, then this is one omission and the capitalisation of the next word, which will be the first word of the next sentence, is a second omission. This is great as you are effectively getting two for the price of one. I only mention this because it is important that you recognise that this is two omissions rather than one (if you see this as only one omission, then not only will you waste time looking for a missing piece of punctuation which is not there, but you may also end up inserting an additional punctuation mark somewhere that is not required). Make sure you make 15 alterations to the text, no more, no less, if you wish to have the best chance of scoring full marks on this section of the test (and scoring full marks here is easily doable).

Please note that this is not a comprehensive guide on how to use punctuation, but more of a quick guide on punctuation to help you pass this section of the test with as little effort as possible.

3.1   Full stops

One of the most common punctuation mistakes concerns the use, or the lack of use of full stops. A full stop is required at the end of every sentence, and it is highly likely that there will be missing full stops in your QTS test. If you have spotted a missing full stop, this is great news, as you will probably also need to capitalise the word immediately following this full stop, meaning that you now have found two punctuation omissions. There may even be a missing full stop at the end of a paragraph, which should be relatively easy to spot. I would recommend that the first thing you do in the punctuation section is to quickly scan every paragraph to see if there are missing full stops at the end of them. If there are, then you have gained your first mark with minimal effort.

Helping people with full stops by telling them that a full stop is needed at the end of a sentence is probably not that helpful, since most people know this already. The problem is understanding what actually makes a sentence.

A sentence is one main idea, thought or feeling, a set of words which is complete in itself, and this set of words must also make sense. It will contain a subject (the person or thing that completes the action, e.g. the teacher, Gary, my mum, he, they etc.) and a verb (the action, or doing word). The sentence may also have an object (the thing the verb is being done to) and it may contain subordinate clauses (additional pieces of information which can be removed and the main clause still makes sense). Without wanting to go into unnecessary detail, here is an example of a sentence:

The dog, who is called Colin, ate the bone.

'The dog' is the subject of the sentence (it is the person / thing that did the eating), 'ate' is the verb (the action word) and 'the bone' is the object since it was the thing that was eaten. The phrase 'who is called Colin' is a subordinate or dependent clause, providing a bit of additional information, but this clause can be removed from the main clause, still leaving us with the complete sentence 'The dog ate the bone.'

Remembering that a sentence is a group of words which makes sense on its own, and which conveys one idea, thought or feeling, see if you can work out what is wrong with this example:

Grange Hill school has five non-negotiable classroom rules if these rules are broken, then students will receive a sanction

This example should be divided into two separate sentences as follows:

Grange Hill school has five non-negotiable classroom rules. If these rules are broken, then students will receive a sanction.

'Grange Hill....rules' makes sense on its own, and is one complete idea which tells the reader how many rules there are at the school. The second sentence 'If.......sanction' also makes sense on its own and is a completely separate idea from the first sentence, since it tells us what happens if one of the five classroom rules is not followed. Since there are two separate ideas, a full stop needs to be inserted between them. A full stop is also required at the very end of the text, after the word 'sanction'.

If you were reading this sentence aloud to someone, you would most certainly pause between the words 'rules' and 'if', and this is another indication that a full stop is required.

However, some people might not use the correct punctuation mark, and might be tempted to use a comma instead of a full stop.

Let's take a look at another example:

The boy swore at the teacher he then kicked his chair over before storming out of the class.

Some people might attempt to correct this sentence by adding a comma between 'teacher' and 'he', but this is wrong:

The boy swore at the teacher, he then kicked his chair over before storming out of the class.

The sentence should be punctuated as follows:

The boy swore at the teacher. He then kicked his chair over before storming out of the class.

In this example, again, there are two complete and separate ideas. The first is the boy swearing at the teacher, and the second is the boy kicking a chair over. 'The boy swore at the teacher' makes sense on its own, so this is a sentence, therefore a full stop is needed. Inserting a full stop here means that the rest of the text from 'he' to 'class' must make sense on its own, which it does.

If you are not certain whether a comma or full stop is required, think how you would read the sentence aloud. Generally, you would take a quick pause for breath when there is a comma, but a full stop allows you to take a much longer break without disrupting the meaning:

The boy was walking down the street but went home as soon as the rain started.

The boy was walking down the street he went home when the rain started.

These sentences should read as follows:

The boy was walking down the street, but went home as soon as the rain started.

The boy was walking down the street. He went home when the rain started.

In the first example, the comma allows you to take a quick pause for breath (or a pause for dramatic effect), but the phrase 'but went home as soon as the rain started' is not a sentence as it does not make sense on its own, so a full stop would be incorrect here.

In the second example, the full stop allows you to take a big pause. You could even go and put the kettle on before coming back to read the next part 'He went home when the rain started'. This is because 'He went home when the rain started' makes sense on its own. It is a sentence, a new idea, so needs to be preceded by a full stop.

3.2　Full stop practice questions

1.　If a student disrupts for a third time, move the student where possible be very clear that you have added a written comment in their planner.

2.　Lend student equipment if they are not equipped for learning if they fail to return equipment, then issue the student with a detention slip.

3.　Grange Hill School is a non-denomination secondary school for boys aged 11 to 18 years girls are welcome in the sixth form.

4.　Stormzy will be coming into school this afternoon to talk about respect it will be a high-energy afternoon.

5.　The school will be closing at 1.20 on Friday students on Free School Meals will be able to collect their meal at break.

6.　Friday 23 November will be a designated INSET day students are not required to come into school on this day.

7.　Please be aware that the autumn term ends on Thursday 20 December students are expected back on Monday the 7th of January.

8.　We welcome girls from all cultures, backgrounds and beliefs the school has a long and distinguished history and has been educating local girls for over 250 years.

9. Our aim is to provide an outstanding education for boys who attend our school we have a strong commitment to the pursuit of learning.

10. It is our belief that boys flourish best in our single-sex environment we have an enviable academic record and are proud of our students' achievements.

11. Members of the Learning Support Team work with subject teachers to develop a range of teaching strategies and resources for use in the classroom they also support individual students in and out of the classroom.

12. The support team also provides assistance for those bilingual learners whose first language is not English support is provided both in the classroom and, when necessary, through withdrawal from normal timetabled lessons.

13. Grange Hill has an extremely successful Sixth Form our primary aim is to ensure that all students experience an academic education of the highest standard.

14. In the Sixth Form, our expectations are high, with senior students expected to operate as role models for students in the lower school this is reflected in the Sixth Form appearance policy.

15. The Sixth Form offers a wide range of Level 3 courses which are studied over two years we offer A levels and BTEC National Diplomas.

16. Students who have not reached 5 A*-C grades at Key Stage 4 can still enter the Sixth Form, taking a one-year Level 2 course upon successful completion, students are encouraged to progress on to the Level 3 courses for a further two years.

17. Our core business is to support the students who study here there are various pastoral structures in place to maximise the potential of our students.

18. As a Sixth Form student, your drive, imagination and energy dictate what happens on a day-to-day basis there is a vast array of opportunities in which to get involved students in the Sixth Form are given a lot more responsibility within the life of the school this involves the appointment of a Head Boy and one or two Deputies, who chair the School Council and can influence the day-to-day working of the school.

19. While there is, of course, a heavy emphasis on working hard, there is a fantastic social life within the Sixth Form the showpiece event is the Summer Ball, a formal event run by the students themselves students also organise inter-consortium activities and social events, including Christmas and Leavers Balls.

20. As part of the Central Consortium, girls are welcomed at Grange Hill although we believe that single-sex education is beneficial through to Key Stage 4, we value having mixed classes in the Sixth Form being a consortium helps us to do this.

3.3   Full stop practice answers

1. If a student disrupts for a third time, move the student where possible. Be very clear that you have added a written comment in their planner.

2. Lend student equipment if they are not equipped for learning. If they fail to return equipment, then issue the student with a detention slip.

3. Grange Hill School is a non-denomination secondary school for boys aged 11 to 18 years. Girls are welcome in the Sixth Form.

4. Stormzy will be coming into school this afternoon to talk about respect. It will be a high-energy afternoon.

5. The school will be closing at 1.20 on Friday. Students on Free School Meals will be able to collect their meal at break.

6. Friday 23 November will be a designated INSET day. Students are not required to come into school on this day.

7. Please be aware that the autumn term ends on Thursday 20 December. Students are expected back on Monday the 7th of January.

8. We welcome girls from all cultures, backgrounds and beliefs. The school has a long and distinguished history and has been educating local girls for over 250 years.

9. Our aim is to provide an outstanding education for boys who attend our school. We have a strong commitment to the pursuit of learning.

10. It is our belief that boys flourish best in our single-sex environment. We have an enviable academic record and are proud of our students' achievements.

11. Members of the Learning Support Team work with subject teachers to develop a range of teaching strategies and resources for use in the classroom. They also support individual students in and out of the classroom.

12. The support team also provides assistance for those bilingual learners whose first language is not English. Support is provided both in the classroom and, when necessary, through withdrawal from normal timetabled lessons.

13. Grange Hill has an extremely successful Sixth Form. Our primary aim is to ensure that all students experience an academic education of the highest standard.

14. In the Sixth Form, our expectations are high, with senior students expected to operate as role models for students in the lower school. This is reflected in the Sixth Form appearance policy.

15. The Sixth Form offers a wide range of Level 3 courses which are studied over two years. We offer A levels and BTEC National Diplomas.

16. Students who have not reached 5 A*- C grades at Key Stage 4 can still enter the Sixth Form, taking a one-year Level 2 course. Upon successful completion, students are encouraged to progress on to the Level 3 courses for a further two years.

17. Our core business is to support the students who study here. There are various pastoral structures in place to maximise the potential of our students.

18. As a Sixth Form student, your drive, imagination and energy dictate what happens on a day-to-day basis. There is a vast array of opportunities in which to get involved. Students in the Sixth Form are given a lot more responsibility within the life of the school. This involves the appointment of a Head Boy and one or two Deputies, who chair the School Council and can influence the day-to-day working of the school.

19. While there is, of course, a heavy emphasis on working hard, there is a fantastic social life within the Sixth Form. The showpiece event is the Summer Ball, a formal event run by the students themselves. Students also organise inter-consortium activities and social events, including Christmas and Leavers Balls.

20. As part of the Central Consortium, girls are welcomed at Grange Hill. Although we believe that single-sex education is beneficial through to Key Stage 4, we value having mixed classes in the Sixth Form. Being a consortium helps us to do this.

3.4   Full Stop Test tips

It is extremely likely that you will need to insert a full stop in the test, perhaps more than once.

Always check that there are full stops in obvious places, such as at the end of every paragraph, and at the end of the piece of text.

You will probably also need to insert a full stop where two sentences have been incorrectly joined together. Remember, a full stop needs to be placed where one idea ends and a second idea starts. Read the text and ask yourself where you would naturally stop: a stop is an indication that you have reached the end of a sentence.

3.5   Commas

The comma is a much misused piece of punctuation. Without wanting to get too caught up in unnecessary detail (although I will illustrate some of the key ways commas should be used below), roughly speaking (very roughly), a comma is used to denote a pause. Think about where you would pause if you were reading a sentence and place commas accordingly. A writer will place commas to tell you where to pause in a sentence so that you can take a breath (essential if you are reading aloud), or to pause so that the overall meaning makes sense.

Consider, where you would pause, if you were reading your sentence, and place commas, accordingly.

In the above example, the writer has put the brakes on too frequently and we do not need to be reminded to pause as frequently as this. Here, the commas have been thrown around like confetti! They have also been placed incorrectly, disrupting the flow and meaning of the sentence. Many people make this common mistake of using too many commas, in the hope that if they put enough commas in a sentence, then at least some will be in the right place.

This is how the above example should have been punctuated:

Consider where you would pause if you were reading your sentence, and place commas accordingly.

If I were reading this sentence aloud, I would naturally pause after the word 'sentence', possibly making use of this comma as an opportunity to take a breath if I were reading aloud, before continuing with the rest of the sentence.

Have you ever had to read a sentence a second time because, at the first attempt, it did not make sense or seemed strange? What goes through your mind when you read the following sentence?

Most of the time travellers worry about their luggage.

Do you not think that the insertion of a comma can completely change the meaning of this sentence?

Most of the time, travellers worry about their luggage.

The insertion of the comma means we should pause after the word 'time'. If there is no comma, we may read the whole sentence without pausing, and end up with quite a different sentence, possibly imagining Doctor Who fretting at an airport terminal because his Samsonite hasn't turned up.

Below are some general rules for comma usage. There is more to the comma than the below, but these are the basics and should be adequate for the purposes of the QTS test.

1. Use a comma to separate items in a list.

   I am going to Tesco this evening to buy eggs, cheese, potatoes and cabbage.

   Each item in the list needs to be separated with a comma, with the exception of the item before the word 'and'. It is quite likely that you will need to do this in the punctuation section, although it is possible you may need to use a semicolon instead of a comma (see section on use of semicolons).

2. Use a comma to separate two adjectives if you could insert the word 'and' between the two adjectives, or if you could reverse the adjectives without affecting the overall meaning. Here is an example:

   The teacher was a tall, old man.

   A comma is required between these two adjectives because the phrase can be written as follows:

   The teacher was an old, tall man.
   The teacher was a tall and old man.

Compare this with the following phrase:

I love hot beef soup.

In this phrase, there is no comma because it would not make sense to put the word 'and' in between the two adjectives. Nor would the phrase make sense if 'hot' and 'beef' were reversed:

I love hot and beef soup.
I love beef hot soup.

3. Use a comma after an introductory word or word group. This could be an introductory adverb such as 'furthermore' or a short phrase like 'at the end of the evening' or 'given the behaviour of the class'. This introductory element adds extra detail and, if you remove it, the rest of the sentence must make sense.

Having analysed this year's results, I see a big dip in the performance of EAL students.

If you remove the introductory phrase 'having analysed this year's results', the rest of the sentence is a complete sentence in its own right, so therefore the use of the comma is correct. Again, if you were reading this sentence aloud, you might pause after the word 'results', and a pause is usually a clue to comma usage, as stated above.

4. Use a comma when you join two sentences together with co-ordinating conjunctions (and, but, or, nor, for, so, yet).

I like cheese.

I don't like milk.

Above are examples of two independent clauses. If we join them together with the word 'but', then a comma must be inserted before the conjunction.

I like cheese, but I don't like milk.

Again, if you were reading this sentence aloud, you might pause after the word 'cheese', and a pause is usually a clue to comma usage, as stated above.

5. Use a comma to interrupt a sentence with additional information, especially if the interruption starts with the words 'who' or 'which'.

The boy, who attends my weekly intervention class, is now starting to make progress.

In this example, the original sentence is "The boy is now starting to make progress". Because we have interrupted this main sentence with extra information about him attending an intervention session, this extra phrase must have a comma both before and after it. Again, if you were reading this sentence aloud, you could pause after the word 'boy' and after the word 'class'.

6. Use a comma if you are joining a dependent clause to an independent clause. An independent clause is a group of words that can stand alone as a sentence and make sense, whereas a dependent clause does not make sense on its own. Here are two examples to illustrate the difference:

Please complete the attached reply slip. This is an independent clause as it can stand alone and make sense.

If you plan to attend Sports Day. This is a dependent clause as it does not make sense on its own. This clause will only make sense when added to another clause.

If the dependent clause comes first, use a comma.
If you plan to attend Sports Day, please complete the attached reply slip.
If the independent clause comes first, no comma is necessary.
Please complete the attached reply slip if you plan to attend Sports Day.

Again, think about where you would pause if you were reading. In the first example, you would probably pause between the words 'Day' and 'please', whereas in the second example, you would read the full sentence without pausing.

7. Use a comma after a salutation (a greeting) in a letter:

Dear Mr Smith,

8. Use a comma before opening speech marks and, in some situations, before closing speech marks (see section on inverted commas).

Make sure you understand the above rules. Remember that if you are uncertain about whether to use a comma or not, thinking about where you would naturally pause when reading the text aloud is a useful starting point.

3.6   Comma practice questions

1. The technology suite which is currently being redeveloped will be ready for September 2019.

2. Until the summer students are expected to wear a smart black blazer at all times.

3. Sadly the boys were outperformed by the girls for the sixth consecutive year.

4. Students will visit the Sagrada Familia Park Güell and of course Camp Nou the home of Barcelona Football Club.

5. In the school canteen you can have sandwiches snacks cooked meals and soft drinks.

6. In the second block of GCSE options students can choose a humanity a language technology or music.

7. Having observed Mr Smith today I have concluded that he needs to improve his use of questioning his behaviour management and his use of AfL.

8. Having paid an initial deposit parents should make arrangements to apply for an EHIC card.

9. As a result more target language needs to be used in modern language lessons.

10. There may however be occasions where a school will be forced to exclude students.

11. George's behaviour in maths is deteriorating making teaching and learning difficult in this lesson.

12. Students are expected to wear knee length grey skirts.

13. Olivia is not working to her potential in lessons nor is she completing homework on time.

14. Ben has received commendations from his teachers so he will be nominated for an end of year award.

15. There are however occasions where a TA may need to intervene.

16. On the other hand Leroy is making excellent progress in rugby even though his attendance in training is sporadic.

17. For example use your seating plan to learn the names of students as soon as possible.

18. Having already received a warning for talking Ben did not modify his behaviour.

19. Simon who is in the top set is an excellent choice for form captain.

20. These results which I am quite proud of are the rewards of all the extra work that I put in last year.

3.7   <u>Comma practice answers</u>

1. The technology suite, which is currently being redeveloped, will be ready for September 2019. *The main sentence has been interrupted with additional information using a 'which' clause, so this extra information needs a comma before and after it* (see rule 5).

2. Until the summer, students are expected to wear a smart, black blazer at all times. *A comma is required after the first introductory word group* (see rule 3). *A second comma is needed to separate the two adjectives that describe the blazer* (see rule 2).

3. Sadly, the boys were outperformed by the girls for the sixth consecutive year. *A comma is required after the first introductory word* (see rule 3).

4. Students will visit the Sagrada Familia, Park Güell and, of course, Camp Nou, the home of Barcelona Football club. *A comma is required to separate the first two items in the list, but note that there is no comma before the word 'and'* (see rule 1). *There is a comma before and after the words 'of course' since there is an interruption* (see rule 5) *and, finally, there is a comma after the word 'Nou' since additional information has been added here* (see rule 5).

5. In the school canteen, you can have sandwiches, snacks, cooked meals and soft drinks. *A comma is required after the first introductory word group* (see rule 3). *Commas are needed to separate items in a list, but note that there is no comma before the word 'and'* (see rule 1).

6. In the second block of GCSE options, students can choose a humanity, a language, technology or music. *A comma is required after the first introductory word group* (see rule 3). *Commas are needed to separate items in a list, but note that there is no comma before the word 'or'* (see rule 1).

7. Having observed Mr Smith today, I have concluded that he needs to improve his use of questioning, his behaviour management and his use of AfL. *A comma is required after the first introductory word group* (see rule 3). *Commas are needed to separate items in a list, but note that there is no comma before the word 'and'* (see rule 1).

8. Having paid an initial deposit, parents should make arrangements to apply for an EHIC card. *A comma is required after the first introductory word group* (see rule 3).

9. As a result, more target language needs to be used in modern language lessons. *A comma is required after the first introductory word group* (see rule 3).

10. There may, however, be occasions where a school will be forced to exclude students. *A comma is required before and after the word 'however' since this is an interruption to the main sentence* (see rule 5).

11. George's behaviour in maths is deteriorating, making teaching and learning difficult in this lesson. *A comma is required after the word 'deteriorating' since additional information is being added* (see rule 5).

12. Students are expected to wear knee length, grey skirts. *A comma is required here to separate two adjectives* (see rule 2).

13. Olivia is not working to her potential in lessons, nor is she completing homework on time. *A comma is required here before the conjunction 'nor'* (see rule 4).

14. Ben has received commendations from his teachers, so he will be nominated for an end of year award. *A comma is required here before the conjunction 'nor'* (see rule 4).

15. There are, however, occasions where a TA may need to intervene. *A comma is required before and after the word 'however' since this is an interruption to the main sentence* (see rule 5).

16. On the other hand, Leroy is making excellent progress in rugby, even though his attendance in training is sporadic. *A comma is required after the first introductory word group* (see rule 3). *A comma is also required after the word 'rugby' since additional information is being added* (see rule 5).

17. For example, use your seating plan to learn the names of students as soon as possible. *A comma is required after the first introductory word group* (see rule 3).

18. Having already received a warning for talking, Ben did not modify his behaviour. *A comma is required after the first introductory word group* (see rule 3). *You could perhaps argue that this is an example of a dependent clause followed by an independent clause* (see rule 6).

19. Simon, who is in the top set, is an excellent choice for form captain. *The main sentence has been interrupted with additional information and a 'who' clause, so this extra information needs a comma before and after it* (see rule 5).

20. These results, which I am quite proud of, are the rewards of all the extra work that I put in last year. *The main sentence has been interrupted with additional information using a 'which' clause, so this extra information needs a comma before and after it* (see rule 5).

3.8   Comma Test tips

It is highly likely that you will be required to insert commas in the text. I would estimate that you will need to add between two and four commas in total.

It is more likely that you will need to use commas to separate items in a list, or to separate two adjectives.

If the text is a letter, you might need to insert a comma at the end of the opening salutation.

In addition to this, it is likely that you will need to use commas after introductory information in sentences, or to separate additional information. Think about where you would pause for breath as a reader, as this is an indication that a comma may be required.

If you think you have punctuated the text to the best of your ability, but you know you are missing a couple to make your tally of 15, then it is quite likely that you have missed some commas.

3.9   Question marks

The use of the question mark is very straightforward, certainly as far as the QTS test is concerned. If the sentence asks a question, then it needs to end with a question mark. In written English, questions are constructed in two ways:

1. The sentence starts with a question word like 'how', 'why', 'who', 'where', 'when', 'what':

How do you tackle the issue of transgenderism in the classroom?

2. The sentence starts with the words 'do, 'does' or 'did':

Do you think your lessons lack pace?

3. The order of the words changes and the verb comes before the subject:

Have you ever considered leaving the profession?

If there are questions in the text which you have to punctuate, it is quite common that the question is the main heading of the text, or possibly a sub-heading. It could also be the opening sentence of a paragraph, where a problem is suggested which is then followed up by some solutions:

Is teacher workload affecting your work-life balance? If this is the case, then here are some pieces of advice for you......

Question marks are used inside speech marks if the words that are being spoken form a question (see below section on how to use speech marks), although it is unlikely that this will be a consideration in the test, since the texts are factual pieces of writing, and not stories with characters. However, it is conceivable that there could be a quote from a person in the form of a rhetorical question.

"Do you genuinely believe that I would exclude poorly-behaved children just because we have an Ofsted inspection?" said Mr Griffiths in response to allegations that many pupils were asked not to attend St Mary's School on the day that Ofsted were planning to visit.

Do not be tempted to add question marks for indirect questions:

The teacher asked if Ofsted would be providing lesson feedback.

3.10   Question Mark Test tips

You may not need to use the question mark in the test, but if you do, it is unlikely that you will use it more than once. If you need to use question marks, they are more likely to be required in the title of the text or in the opening sentence of a paragraph.

3.11   Colons

Understanding how to use a colon correctly is not easy. However, let's make things as easy as possible with just a very brief explanation in terms of how you are expected to use a colon in the QTS test. In the literacy test, a colon is used before a list, and all the items that make up this list come after this colon (all the items in the list subsequently need to be separated by commas or semicolons – see sections on comma and semicolon use). Here is an example of a sentence which has a colon:

These are the field events that the pupils can take part in this year: hammer, shot put, discus, javelin, high jump, long jump, triple jump and pole vault.

In this example, there is a list of field events, so a colon is required before the start of this list (notice too how each item in the list has a comma after it, with the exception of the final item).

You might also see colons being used where there are paragraph titles / headings followed underneath by descriptions / clarifications. In these texts, it is highly likely that you will see other paragraph headings / sub-headings followed by colons, so all you have to do is spot that the pattern is consistent throughout the entire text:

Tennis:

Boys to wear white T-shirt, white shorts, school socks and trainers / plimsols

Girls to wear white T-shirt, white shorts or skirt, school socks and trainers / plimsols

Football

Boys to wear red school football shirt, white shorts, school socks and studded boots

Girls to wear yellow school football shirt, white shorts, school socks and astro trainers

In this example, there is a colon after 'tennis' followed by a description of tennis clothing, but there is no colon after the word 'football', so add a colon here to follow the previously established pattern. Always check for consistency in the text!

3.12   Colon practice questions

(Other punctuation will need to be added to these examples)

1. You may be required to bring many things sleeping bags pans utensils and warm clothing.

2. For next lesson, students will need to bring in the following items flour margarine sugar and vanilla essence.

3. We will be climbing the following mountains to raise funds for Children in Need Snowdon Ben Nevis and Scafell Pike.

4. These are the students who are on the shortlist for Student of the Year Martin Wheeler Ciara Smith Caroline Sargeant and David Thornley.

5. Abdullah Quershi gained a grade 9 in these subjects maths English IT French and triple science.

6. In the GCSE maths exam, you will need the following equipment pen pencil rubber calculator ruler protractor and a pair of compasses.

7. You need to know these verb tenses for the GCSE Spanish exam the present tense the past tense the future tense the conditional tense and the imperfect tense.

8. These British values need to be addressed in every assembly this year democracy rule of law individual liberty and mutual respect.

3.13   Colon practice answers

1. You may be required to bring many things: sleeping bags, pans, utensils and warm clothing.

2. For next lesson, students will need to bring in the following items: flour, margarine, sugar and vanilla essence.

3. We will be climbing the following mountains to raise funds for Children in Need: Snowdon, Ben Nevis and Scafell Pike.

4. These are the students who are on the shortlist for Student of the Year: Martin Wheeler, Ciara Smith, Caroline Sargeant and David Thonnley.

5. Abdullah Quershi gained a grade 9 in these subjects: maths, English, IT, French and triple science.

6. In the GCSE maths exam, you will need the following equipment: pen, pencil, rubber, calculator, ruler, protractor and a pair of compasses.

7. You need to know these verb tenses for the GCSE Spanish exam: the present tense, the past tense, the future tense, the conditional tense and the imperfect tense.

8. These British values need to be addressed in every assembly this year: democracy, rule of law, individual liberty and mutual respect.

3.14   Colon Test tips

Don't overthink the colon! In the QTS test, if you are required to use a colon, you are only likely to use it to introduce a list. It could also be required after a word or phrase as a sub-heading or bullet point, but this should be obvious since you should see other sub-headings or bullet points punctuated in the same way.

3.15   Semicolons

Semicolons are also very difficult to use, but as far as the QTS literacy test is concerned, you will only encounter them, if you encounter them at all, in lists.   I have mentioned in the comma section above that when you are writing lists, each item should be separated by a comma.

Here are my recommendations for House Captain: Bob, Gary, Fred and Steve.

The list is introduced by a colon and the items in the list are separated by commas.   The items in the list are:

Bob

Gary

Fred

Steve

What if the list was as follows?

Bob, Turner House

Gary, Adam House

Fred, Brunel House

Steve, Shackleton House

The list would now read:

Here are my recommendations for House Captain: Bob, Turner House, Gary, Adam House, Fred, Brunel House and Steve, Shackleton House.

This list is very messy, and possibly confusing, as there are so many commas. You could also argue that 'Turner House' looks like one of the recommendations for House Captain.

When items in the list already contain commas, you should use semicolons rather than commas to separate the items.

Therefore the above example should read as follows:

Here are my recommendations for House Captain: Bob, Turner House; Gary, Adam House; Fred, Brunel House; and Steve, Shackleton House.

Generally speaking, if the list is slightly complicated you can justify the use of a semicolon over a comma. Note too that before the final 'and' in the list, there is another placement of a semicolon (in a list using commas, you would not use an additional comma before the final item), but it is unlikely that you will need to position a semicolon in this part of a list in the test. Here is another example of a complicated list:

A few items are required for this trip: a large rucksack for all of the equipment; a selection of ropes of various thicknesses; specialist rock-climbing shoes with rubber soles; and a head torch with extra batteries.

As I am sure you can appreciate, this list is much more complicated than the following list, which would only require commas:

A few items are required for this trip: a large rucksack, a selection of ropes, specialist rock-climbing shoes and a head torch.

I can imagine that you are asking yourself the question, "At what stage does a simple list become a complicated list?" Don't worry about it! In the QTS test, you will know to use semicolons rather than commas because it is likely that you will see other items in the list separated by semicolons. As I have said before, always check for consistency. If you see commas in a list, don't start adding semicolons and vice versa.

3.16   Semicolon practice questions

These examples are more challenging than the QTS test as there is a lot of punctuation missing. In the actual test, there will be far less missing punctuation than this, and the punctuation they have included will guide you as to how to complete the rest.

1. In today's meeting we have the following attendees Gary Smith University of Bristol Simon Jones University of Warwick Gemma Ledbury University of Hull and Steve Nichol University of Liverpool.

2. These are the boys that should go on report at the start of the summer term Reece James 23 negatives Ibrahim Abdullah 17 negatives Lindrit Emin 14 negatives and Nabil Syed 12 negatives.

3. This is the proposal for the upcoming trip to Paris The Eiffel Tower an opportunity to take photos of this famous landmark the Louvre a chance to see the famous Mona Lisa the Catacombs a chance to see an underground burial site and Notre Dame a spectacular Gothic church.

4. We will need the following equipment for the Duke of Edinburgh expedition tent which needs to be waterproof sleeping bag which should be suitable for temperatures down to 10 degrees first aid kit waterproofs which should have taped seams and walking boots which should be waterproof and comfortable.

5. This is a breakdown of what was collected for Children in Need by Year 7 7A £34 7B £76 7C £35 and 7D £64.

6. The following offences will result in a student being placed in isolation bringing the school into disrepute smoking including use of e-cigarettes criminal damage theft verbal abuse to staff and inappropriate use of mobile phones.

7. All our school rewards are issued as follows stamps recorded in planners by subject teachers reward postcards sent home on termly basis phone calls home made when pupils have achieved 50 stamps and certificates issued in end of term assemblies.

8. These are the classroom non-negotiables arrive on time be equipped for learning respect teachers by doing as you are asked, first time every time always do your best put your hand up and wait for permission to speak and always do your homework

9. This is step 4 of the behaviour system write third comment in planner fill in yellow detention slip enter a negative on school database issue work to student and send student to withdrawal room.

10. During form time we expect tutors to check planners discuss the thought of the day conduct uniform checks read relevant notices select a pupil of the week and have conversations with students who are routinely late.

3.17　Semicolon practice answers

1. In today's meeting we have the following attendees: Gary Smith, University of Bristol; Simon Jones, University of Warwick; Gemma Ledbury, University of Hull; and Steve Nichol, University of Liverpool.

2. These are the boys that should go on report at the start of the summer term: Reece James, 23 negatives; Ibrahim Abdullah, 17 negatives; Lindrit Emin, 14 negatives; and Nabil Syed, 12 negatives.

3. This is the proposal for the upcoming trip to Paris: The Eiffel Tower, an opportunity to take photos of this famous landmark; the Louvre, a chance to see the famous Mona Lisa; the Catacombs, a chance to see an underground burial site; and Notre Dame, a spectacular Gothic church.

4. We will need the following equipment for the Duke of Edinburgh expedition: tent, which needs to be waterproof; sleeping bag, which should be suitable for temperatures down to 10 degrees; first aid kit; waterproofs, which should have taped seams; and walking boots, which should be waterproof and comfortable.

5. This is a breakdown of what was collected for Children in Need by Year 7: 7A, £34; 7B, £76; 7C, £35; and 7D, £64.

6. The following offences will result in a student being placed in isolation: bringing the school into disrepute; smoking, including use of e-cigarettes; criminal damage; theft; verbal abuse to staff; and inappropriate use of mobile phones.

7. All our school rewards are issued as follows: stamps recorded in planners by subject teachers; reward postcards sent home on termly basis; phone calls home made when pupils have achieved 50 stamps; and certificates issued in end of term assemblies.

8. These are the classroom non-negotiables: arrive on time; be equipped for learning; respect teachers by doing as you are asked, first time every time; always do your best; put your hand up and wait for permission to speak; and always do your homework

9. This is step 4 of the behaviour system: write third comment in planner; fill in yellow detention slip; enter a negative on school database; issue work to student; and send student to withdrawal room.

10. During form time we expect tutors to: check planners; discuss the thought of the day; conduct uniform checks; read relevant notices; select a pupil of the week; and have conversations with students who are routinely late.

3.18   Semicolon Test tips

The semicolon can be difficult to use, but in the test it will be easy. If you need to use a semicolon, then it will be in a list. Use a semicolon when there is no punctuation mark between items in a list, but only if all other items in the list are separated by semicolons. Simply continue the pattern.

3.19   <u>Speech marks (double quotation marks)</u>

When you are writing, speech marks need to surround only the words that have been spoken by the person in the text. One set of speech marks needs to be inserted at the beginning of what was spoken, and a second set at the end of what was spoken. You will see numerous examples of speech marks in novels since there will no doubt be lots of direct speech between a story's characters. In the skills test, you will not be asked to punctuate an extract from the Da Vinci code, where there is dialogue between characters, but you might be asked to punctuate a short article about education in which there could be a quote from someone.

It also seems likely that, if you are required to use speech marks in the test, then one set of speech marks will already be given. Whenever you see speech marks in the text, immediately check to see if the speech marks are complete (in other words, is there a set of speech marks at the beginning of what was said and a second set at the end of what was said?). It is highly likely that if there is reported speech in the text, then one of the speech marks will be missing, and it is more likely that the second set of speech marks will be missing than the first set.

"We need to ensure that pupils from all social classes have the opportunity to succeed in school a government minister said.

In the example above, we can see that there is only one set of speech marks, so we know that we need to insert a second set somewhere, but where? We know the words that the government minister said. He said a total of 17 words, the first being the word 'we' and the final word being 'school', therefore the second set of speech marks needs to be after the word 'school'.

If the second set of speech marks is missing, then you may need to insert an additional punctuation mark before the closing speech marks, and this is the trickier part. You should insert a question mark if what was said was a question, an exclamation mark (although let's eliminate this as a possibility since you do not have the option of inserting exclamation marks in the literacy test), a comma or a full stop. In the above example, what was said was not a question, so we now need to choose between a comma and a full stop. Because the sentence continues with the words 'the government minister said' we use a comma, not a full stop. So the sentence should be punctuated as follows:

"We need to ensure that pupils from all social classes have the opportunity to succeed in school," a government minister said.

So there are two marks available here, one for the second set of speech marks and one for the comma before the speech marks.

Let's take a look if the sentence given had been presented like this:

A government minister said "We need to ensure that pupils from all social classes have the opportunity to succeed in school

Here, we again need to put a set of speech marks after the word 'school', as before. However, in this example, 'school' is the final word of the sentence (and is not followed by 'the government minister said') so here we would use a full stop. Remember, that the full stop, comma or question mark needs to come before the closing speech marks.

However, in this example we would also need to put a comma after the word 'said' so the example would be punctuated as follows:

A government minister said, "We need to ensure that pupils from all social classes have the opportunity to succeed in school."

To sum up this quite complicated point, this list should clarify:

1. Identify if it is the opening speech marks (the first set) which are missing or the closing speech marks (the second set).

2. If it is the closing speech marks that are missing (more likely), add the speech marks immediately after the final word that the person said. In addition, add a comma between the final word that was spoken and the closing speech marks if the final spoken word is not the final word of the overall sentence, or add a full stop between the final word that was spoken and the closing speech marks if the final word that the person said is also the final word of the overall sentence.

3. If it is the first set of speech marks that are missing, then simply insert an opening set of speech marks. If the speech marks are preceded by a phrase like 'Bob said', then you need a comma after the word 'said'. Remember too that the first word inside the speech marks needs to be capitalised.

Here are several examples for you to practise with. In these examples, there is no punctuation at all, which makes it even more challenging. As I mentioned above, it is more likely that, if you need to insert speech marks, you will only need to insert one set because the other set (probably the opening speech marks) will already be given.

3.17 Speech marks practice questions

1. One of my colleagues said to me if you had looked after your form group better, these problems wouldn't have arisen

2. The chances that they would do that on their own is negligible said Carrie Herbert, a former teacher.

3. We have saved children from ending up in gangs, and families from having breakdowns Herbert says.

4. Saunders says do we want them to leave with no self-esteem whatsoever

5. In response, Ferguson, the headteacher says all children at this school will be given the opportunity to succeed, so excluding them is not helpful to them in the long term

6. One small step for man, one giant leap for mankind were the famous words spoken by Neil Armstrong.

7. The headteacher started the assembly by saying the man who says he can, and the man who says he can't, are usually both correct

8. At the conference Chad Grylls said in its current state, what we call education is leading humanity towards extinction

9. Learning is not the product of teaching said Mr Holt it is the product of the activity of learners

10. Mr Simmonds addressed the audience at Open Evening and, controversially, proclaimed a child educated only at school is an uneducated child

3.18   Speech marks practice answers

1. One of my colleagues said to me, "If you had looked after your form group better, these problems wouldn't have arisen." *An opening set of speech marks is required before the word 'if' and a closing set after the word 'arisen'. The word 'if' requires capitalisation since it is the first word that was spoken. A comma is required after the phrase 'said to me'. A full stop is required before the closing speech marks because 'arisen' is the final word in the sentence.*

2. "The chances that they would do that on their own is negligible," said Carrie Herbert, a former teacher. *An opening set of speech marks is required before the word 'the' and a closing set after the word 'negligible'. A comma is required before the closing speech marks because 'negligible' is not the final word in the sentence.*

3. "We have saved children from ending up in gangs, and families from having breakdowns," says Herbert. *An opening set of speech marks is required before the word 'we' and a closing set after the word 'breakdowns'. A comma is required after the word 'breakdowns' because 'breakdowns' is not the final word in the sentence.*

4. Saunders says, "Do we want them to leave with no self-esteem whatsoever?" *An opening set of speech marks is required before the word 'do' and a closing set after the word 'whatsoever'. The word 'do' requires capitalisation since it is the first word that was spoken. A comma is required after 'says'. A question mark is required before the closing set of speech marks since this is clearly a question and not a statement.*

5. In response, Ferguson, the headteacher says, "All children at this school will be given the opportunity to succeed, so excluding them is not helpful to them in the long term." *An opening set of speech marks is required before the word 'all' and a closing set after the word 'term'. The word 'all' requires capitalisation since it is the first word that was spoken. A comma is required after 'says'. A full stop needs to be added before the closing speech marks because 'term' is the final word in the sentence.*

6. "One small step for man, one giant leap for mankind," were the famous words spoken by Neil Armstrong. *An opening set of speech marks is required before the word 'one' and a closing set after the word 'mankind'. A comma is required after the word 'mankind' since 'mankind' is not the final word in the sentence.*

7. The headteacher started the assembly by saying, "The man who says he can, and the man who says he can't, are usually both correct." *An opening set of speech marks is required before the word 'the' and a closing set after the word 'correct'. A comma needs to be added after the word 'saying'. The word 'the' needs to be capitalised since it is the first word that was spoken. A full stop is required after the word 'correct' since it is the final word of the sentence.*

8. At the conference, Chad Grylls said, "In its current state, what we call education is leading humanity towards extinction." *An opening set of speech marks is required before the word 'in' and a closing set after the word extinction'. A comma is required after the word 'said'. The word 'in' needs to be capitalised since it is the first word that was spoken. A full stop is required before the closing speech marks since 'extinction' is the final word of the sentence.*

9. "Learning is not the product of teaching," said Mr Holt, "It is the product of the activity of learners." *An opening set of speech marks is required before the word 'learning' and a closing set after the word 'teaching'. A comma is required before the closing speech marks since 'teaching' is not the final word of the sentence. A second opening set of speech marks is required before the word 'it' and a closing set after the word 'learners'. The word 'it' needs to be capitalised as it is the first word that is spoken in this group of spoken words. A comma is required after the phrase 'said Mr Holt'. A full stop is required before the second closing speech marks because 'learners' is the final word of the sentence.*

10. Mr Simmonds addressed the audience at Open Evening and, controversially, proclaimed, "A child educated only at school is an uneducated child." *An opening set of speech marks is required before the word 'a' and a closing set after the word 'child'. The word 'a' needs to be capitalised as it was the first word that was spoken. A comma needs to be inserted after the word 'proclaimed'. A full stop needs to be added after the word 'child' since this is the final word of the sentence.*

3.19   Speech marks Test tips

In the test, you may not need to use speech marks but, if you do, you will probably only need to add it once.   You may also need to add other punctuation marks once you have added any missing speech marks.

You will know if speech marks are missing because one set, either the opening or closing speech marks, will already be given. All you need to do is work out where the spoken part of the sentence starts and ends.

If you are adding opening speech marks, then you need a comma before the speech marks (unless the sentence starts with speech marks), and the first word of the spoken part needs to have a capital letter.

If you are adding closing speech marks, remember that the speech marks need to go after the comma, full stop, question mark or exclamation mark (and it is possible that these commas, full stops and question marks may be absent too).

3.20 Inverted commas (single quotation marks)

Similar to speech marks, inverted commas come in pairs, so in the test, if you see one solitary inverted comma, you simply need to work out where the second inverted comma belongs. These inverted commas will be used to highlight the titles of books, films, plays etc. Here is a quick and easy example:

In year 10, all students will be required to study the novel 'An Inspector Calls. In year 11, they will move on to the Shakespeare play Macbeth'.

It is unlikely that you will have two examples of missing inverted commas in the text, but I have included two examples in one sentence simply to illustrate the point.

The sentence should read:

In year 10, all students will be required to study the novel 'An Inspector Calls'. In year 11, they will move on to the Shakespeare play 'Macbeth'.

Inverted commas simply require an eagle eye for detail. If you spot one inverted comma, check to see if there is a second one.

Note too, that full stops are placed outside the inverted commas since full stops are not part of the actual title. The same applies for any other punctuation marks (commas, exclamation marks, question marks, colons etc.). If they are not part of the title itself, then they do not appear inside the quotation marks.

Inverted commas can also be used to emphasise a word. This might be because the word is technical, unfamiliar or, more likely in the test, ironic:

John submitted his 'art' project late.

In this example, the word 'art' has been placed in inverted commas to create a sense of irony about John's ability as an artist. Clearly the project that John submitted is far from what the teacher deems to be 'art' in the real sense of the word. Can you imagine someone saying this sentence in an ironic way? Could you imagine the teacher even making an air quotation marks sign with his fingers when he says the word 'art'?

Some people are not sure when to use double or single quotation marks, but I wouldn't be too concerned about this in the test. Let's just assume that for the purposes of this test that the double quotation mark is used for direct speech, and single quotation marks for titles. Again, take your cues from what punctuation has already been given. If a title happens to have double rather than single quotation marks in front of it (I do not think this would be likely in the test as this would be incorrect), then it would be logical to use double quotations marks after it in order to keep the consistency.

Do not confuse inverted commas with apostrophes. Apostrophes are used for contractions (hadn't) or for possession (Steve's gloves). See my explanation of apostrophes for more guidance on this.

Here are a few quick examples, although these should be really easy!

3.21   Inverted comma practice questions

1. In order to boost some of our under-achieving pupils, the English department will be running an Easter invention session on King Lear.

2. In a recent article in The Independent, schools are being severely affected by budget cuts.

3. I think that all the students in the food technology group would benefit from watching The Great British Bake Off and Masterchef.

4. The latest Anthony Horowitz novel Scared to Death is now available in the library.

5. I recommend that all students read You are Awesome by Matthew Syed.

6. Tickets for Private Peaceful will be available for sale from Monday.

7. The year 11s are going to undertake a business project, very similar to one of the tasks seen on The Apprentice.

8. I am looking forward to tasting Paula's delicious brownies in food technology this afternoon!

9. Gary said that he was working but, to me, it looked like he was wasting time.

10. The handwriting in this exercise book is described by Luca as neat.

3.22 Inverted comma practice answers

1. In order to boost some of our under-achieving pupils, the English department will be running an Easter invention session on 'King Lear'.

2. In a recent article in 'The Independent', schools are being severely affected by budget cuts.

3. I think that all the students in the food technology group would benefit from watching 'The Great British Bake Off' and 'Masterchef'.

4. The latest Anthony Horowitz novel 'Scared to Death' is now available in the library.

5. I recommend that all students read 'You are Awesome' by Matthew Syed.

6. Tickets for 'Private Peaceful' will be available for sale from Monday.

7. The year 11s are going to undertake a business project, very similar to one of the tasks seen on 'The Apprentice'.

8. I am looking forward to tasting Paula's 'delicious' brownies in food technology this afternoon! *(Sarcastic use of 'delicious'. Clearly Paula has a reputation for not making very tasty brownies. You could also justify putting the inverted commas around the word 'brownies'. This would mean that they were definitely delicious, but perhaps not recognisable as brownies.)*

9. Gary said that he was 'working' but, to me, it looked like he was wasting time. *(Sarcastic use of the word 'working'. Gary's definition of what work is is clearly very different to what the speaker believes.)*

10. The handwriting in this exercise book is described by Luca as 'neat'. *(Sarcastic use of the word 'neat'. Luca's definition of what neat handwriting is is clearly very different to what the speaker believes.)*

Questions 8 – 10 are quite hard, and do make sense without the need for inverted commas. Remember that in the actual test, you have the added benefit of context, and one of the two inverted commas will invariably be given, meaning that a missing inverted comma around a word for emphasis will be much easier to spot.

3.23   Inverted comma Test tips

In the test, you may need to use an inverted comma, but it is unlikely to appear in every test. The lack of inverted comma should be easy to spot because they appear as a set of two, and you will probably just see one of them, so all you have to do is work out where the missing one belongs. Inverted commas belong before, and after, titles of plays, books and films.

You may need to put inverted commas around a phrase or word to draw attention to it, although this is less likely. Again, one of the inverted commas will be provided, so you simply need to work out where the other one belongs.

Do not confuse inverted commas and apostrophes. It is only inverted commas that come in pairs: apostrophes appear on their own.

3.24 <u>Apostrophes</u>

Apostrophes are extremely misused in the English language. Apostrophes should never be used when making a word plural! An apostrophe in a plural is probably the most common grammatical error made in the English language. It is not acceptable to write, "This shop sells sweet's and chocolate bar's....'. In this example both the nouns 'sweet' and 'bar' being used in their plural form, so 'sweets' and 'bars' is correct. Do not be tempted to add apostrophes to any plural words in your literacy test!

The apostrophe is used for contractions (a word which has been shortened and combines two words) and replaces a missing letter. Here are the most common contractions:

- From the verb 'to be': I'm / you're / he's / she's / it's / we're / they're / that's / who's

- From the verb 'to have': I've / you've / he's / she's / we've / they've

- For the word 'not': don't / doesn't / didn't / can't / won't / shouldn't / wouldn't / couldn't / mightn't / mustn't / wasn't / weren't / haven't / hasn't / hadn't / isn't / aren't

- For the word 'have': would've / could've / should've / might've / must've

- For the word 'will': I'll / you'll / he'll /she'll / it'll / we'll / they'll

- For the word 'would': I'd / you'd / he'd /she'd / we'd / they'd

- For the word 'had': I'd / you'd / he'd / she'd / we'd / they'd

The apostrophe is also used to indicate possession:

Simon's behaviour (the behaviour of Simon) *has been deteriorating since the start of the school year.*

The student's work (the work of the student) *was below the required standard.*

If the noun (item, object, thing) belongs to a singular person, then the apostrophe goes before the letter 's', but if the noun belongs to more than one person, then the apostrophe needs to go after the letter 's':

The boy's behaviour (the behaviour of the boy (singular)) *last week was disgraceful.*

The boys' behaviour (the behaviour of the boys (plural)) *last week was disgraceful.*

Be careful with irregular plurals such as 'men's coats' (the coats of men), 'women's rights' (the rights of women), 'children's behaviour' (the behaviour of children). (Never write ' mens' ' or ' childrens' '.)

The apostrophe is *not* used in these words: yours, his, hers, its (if 'it' means 'belonging to it' and not 'it is'), ours, theirs, but it is in one's (belonging to one).

3.25 Apostrophe practice questions

1. The school constantly monitor students attendance levels.

2. We ask that communication is maintained through the use of the students planner on a weekly basis and are always keen to address any issues which parents/carers may have. Should any students behaviour or progress become of concern, we will ensure that the issues are addressed.

3. The two principal components that drive our schools ethos are our commitment to academic success and to developing the individual.

4. The governments planned changes do not, for the time being, apply to Extended BTEC National Diploma courses.

5. Pastoral care is central to students progress and learning at Grange Hill.

6. In addition to places reserved for the schools own pupils, the governors propose to admit a minimum of 15 external students annually to its Sixth Form.

7. Appeals against an unsuccessful application should be made to the Schools Admissions Secretary who will arrange for an Independent Appeals Committee to hear the appeal.

8. Dont think you wont be caught; there are many ways to detect plagiarism. Remember, its your qualification so it needs to be your own work.

9. Its a shame that our school, despite its best efforts, cant find ways to improve certain students attitudes.

10. The childrens books had been marked according to school policy.

3.26 Apostrophe practice answers

1. The school constantly monitor students' *(the attendance of students)* attendance levels.

2. We ask that communication is maintained through the use of the student's planner *(the planner of the student)* on a weekly basis and are always keen to address any issues which parents/carers may have. Should any student's behaviour *(the behaviour of any student)* or progress become of concern, we will ensure that the issues are addressed.

3. The two principal components that drive our school's ethos *(the ethos of our school)* are our commitment to academic success and to developing the individual.

4. The government's planned changes *(the planned changes of the government)* do not, for the time being, apply to Extended BTEC National Diploma courses.

5. Pastoral care is central to students' progress *(the progress of students)* and learning at Grange Hill.

6. In addition to places reserved for the school's own pupils *(the pupils of the school)*, the governors propose to admit a minimum of 15 external students annually to its Sixth Form.

7. Appeals against an unsuccessful application should be made to the School's Admissions Secretary *(the Admissions Secretary of the school)* who will arrange for an Independent Appeals Committee to hear the appeal.

8. Don't think you won't be caught; there are many ways to detect plagiarism. Remember, it's *(contracted form of 'it is')* your qualification so it needs to be your own work.

9. It's *(contracted form of 'it is')* a shame that our school, despite its *(no apostrophe needed)* best efforts, can't find ways to improve certain students' attitudes *(the attitudes of certain students)*.

10. The children's books *(the books of the children)* had been marked according to school policy.

3.27 Apostrophe Test tips

It is highly likely that you will need to add at least one apostrophe in the test. You are likely to have to insert an apostrophe where it has been omitted in a contraction (won't / can't etc.) or where there is an indication of possession. Be careful with the positioning of the possessive apostrophe where the noun is in the plural form (the boys' books = the books of the boys, the boy's books = the books of the boy).

Do not use apostrophes to make a noun plural!

3.28   Brackets (parentheses)

Opening bracket = (

Closing bracket =)

In the same way that inverted commas and speech marks should be easy to spot, brackets should also be easy. Brackets come in sets and, should you need to select brackets in the punctuation section, then it is likely that you will be given one of the brackets, meaning you simply need to work out where the other missing bracket belongs. If you are given an opening bracket, make sure you select a closing bracket and vice versa. It is highly unlikely that you would be asked to insert both an opening and a closing bracket, since the decision to use brackets or to not use brackets can be a matter of personal taste. However, if you see that brackets have been opened, they have to be closed, and if there is a closed bracket, there also needs to be an opening bracket.

Brackets are used to include extra information which isn't essential to the main point of the sentence. It could be an aside, or a quick phrase or short sentence to clarify something. You may have seen examples of this in the text (but if you haven't, then here is one for you right now!).

Here is an example of a sentence that could be part of the punctuation section in the test:

At Grange Hill School, our expectation is that all forms of low-level disruption (talking, fidgeting, pen-tapping, swinging on chairs, staring out of the window should be challenged by classroom teachers.

In this sentence, we first of all need to identify what is inside the brackets. In this example, inside the brackets are various descriptors of low-level disruption. All we need to do is work out when the low-level disruption examples stop before the sentence resumes. The final descriptor of low-level disruption is 'staring out of a window' so the closing bracket needs to come immediately after this.

At Grange Hill School, our expectation is that all forms of low-level disruption (talking, fidgeting, pen-tapping, swinging on chairs, staring out of the window) should be challenged by classroom teachers.

If you remove the bracketed section completely, the sentence needs to make sense, which it does:

At Grange Hill School, our expectation is that all forms of low-level disruption should be challenged by classroom teachers.

If you remove the bracketed section and it does not make sense, then you have not put the brackets in the correct place:

At Grange Hill School, our expectation is that all forms of low-level disruption (talking, fidgeting, pen-tapping, swinging on chairs, staring out of the window should be challenged) by classroom teachers.

If we remove the bracketed section, we are left with:

At Grange Hill School, our expectation is that all forms of low-level disruption by classroom teachers.

Since this sentence makes no sense when the bracketed section has been removed, this tells us that we have not positioned the brackets correctly.

3.29 Bracket practice questions

1. For the next charity drive, we would like all students to bring food items milk, jam, sugar, tea, coffee to help the homeless.

2. We would like all teachers of EBacc subjects English, maths, MFL, geography, history and science to attend the after school training session on Thursday.

3. Hassan new pupil from Somalia will need support in lessons since English is not his first language.

4. At Grange Hill School, pupils who represent the school for sport football, rugby, hockey, and athletics may receive a participation award at the end of term.

5. Education providers primary school, secondary schools, academies, pupil referral units will all be affected by the latest budget cuts.

6. Michael Gove the former Minister for Education made many controversial decisions which have negatively affected schools in our area.

7. The borough of Lewisham always seems to outperform other local boroughs Lambeth, Croydon, Southwark, and Bromley in terms of academic attainment.

8. Gary Smith winner of the Headmaster's Cup has turned down the offer of going to Cambridge and is going to read English at Durham.

9. We would like all members of staff to log all negative behaviours lack of planner, punctuality, uniform violations, low-level disruption, defiant conduct, aggressive behaviour, rudeness to staff on the new behaviour database.

10. Mrs Acaster local resident is always coming to the school to complain about the behaviour of our pupils at the end of the school day.

3.30 Bracket practice answers

1. For the next charity drive, we would like all students to bring food items (milk, jam, sugar, tea, coffee) to help the homeless. *In this example, examples of food items are put inside brackets to clarify the types of food items that the students are expected to bring in. Remove the bracketed part and the sentence still makes sense.*

2. We would like all teachers of EBacc subjects (English, maths, MFL, geography, history and science) to attend the after school training session on Thursday. *In this example, the bracketed section lists which subjects are included for the EBacc, in case there are teachers who are not aware what the EBacc includes. Remove the bracketed part and the sentence still makes sense.*

3. Hassan (new pupil from Somalia) will need support in lessons since English is not his first language. *In this example, clarification of who Hassan is is included in the bracketed section, in case there are teachers who need reminding who this student is. Remove the bracketed part and the sentence still makes sense.*

4. At Grange Hill School, pupils who represent the school for sport (football, rugby, hockey, and athletics) may receive a participation award at the end of term. *In this example, examples of the different school sports that the school participates in are listed for the benefit of the reader who may not be fully aware of the school's sport offering. Remove the bracketed part and the sentence still makes sense.*

5. Education providers (primary school, secondary schools, academies, pupil referral units) will all be affected by the latest budget cuts. *In this example, examples of the different types of educational providers are listed for the benefit of the reader who may not know which providers are going to be affected by the budget cuts. Remove the bracketed part and the sentence still makes sense.*

6. Michael Gove (the former Minister for Education) made many controversial decisions which have negatively affected schools in our area. *In this example, additional information clarifying who Michael Gove is is inserted in the brackets in case the reader has not heard of Michael Gove before. Remove the bracketed part and the sentence still makes sense.*

7. The borough of Lewisham always seems to outperform other local boroughs (Lambeth, Croydon, Southwark, and Bromley) in terms of academic attainment. *In this example, other London boroughs local to Lewisham are listed to highlight which ones Lewisham has outperformed. Remove the bracketed part and the sentence still makes sense.*

8. Gary Smith (winner of the Headmaster's Cup) has turned down the offer of going to Cambridge and is going to read English at Durham. *In this example, additional information about Gary Smith has been added. Here the bracketed section just adds weight to the fact that Gary Smith is clearly a very hard-working, intelligent student and reminds the reader who Gary Smith is, in case the reader was not sure who he was. Remove the bracketed part and the sentence still makes sense.*

9. We would like all members of staff to log all negative behaviours (lack of planner, punctuality, uniform violations, low-level disruption, defiant conduct, aggressive behaviour, rudeness to staff) on the new behaviour database. *In this example, examples of negative behaviours are put inside brackets to clarify the types of offence that are considered to be negative. Remove the bracketed part and the sentence still makes sense.*

10. Three boys in year 8 have been excluded, of which two (Reece Martins and Simon McPherson) are being questioned by police. *In this example, the names of the two boys who are going to be questioned by the police have been included in the bracketed section in case the reader wants to know their identity. Remove the bracketed part and the sentence still makes sense. You could justify the use of a comma here, but in the QTS test, you are likely to know to use brackets rather than commas because one of the sets of brackets will be provided for you.*

3.31 Bracket Test tips

In the test, you might need to add an opening or closing bracket. This will be obvious because brackets come in sets of two and you should spot quite easily that one of them is missing. All you need to do is work out what should be inside the brackets and position the missing bracket accordingly. Remember that if you were to completely remove the entire bracketed section from the sentence, the sentence needs to make sense.

3.32 Capitals

There must always be a reason for a capital letter. If you can't think of a reason, then keep the word in lower case.

A capital letter is always required to start a sentence and for proper nouns. Proper nouns include names of people, names of places (countries, cities, districts, planets), nationalities, languages, names of schools, names of companies, days of the week, months of the year, holidays (Easter, Christmas), titles of books, films, plays, songs.

Titles can be difficult to capitalise but, generally speaking, you should capitalise the first and last words of a title as well as any important words in between ('The Boy in the Striped Pyjamas'). Worrying about which words in a title are important for capitalisation purposes is likely to be beyond the scope of the QTS test.

You do not require capital letter for school subjects (science, maths, history), unless it is a language (French, Spanish, English) or it is an acronym (PSHE, DT).

You do not require capital letters for words like 'school', 'headteacher', 'borough', but these words would be capitalised in a title:

East Finchley Primary School
The Headteacher Mr Ferguson
The London Borough of Lewisham

In the QTS test, it is more likely that you will be capitalising a letter because you have already had to insert a missing full stop, but it is possible that there might be a missing capital letter at the start of a sentence / paragraph, or a missing capital letter in a title (although unlikely that you will need to capitalise more than one word in a title).

3.33 Capitals practice questions

1. pupil attainment is better in some parts of the Uk than others.

2. in the london borough of lewisham, there are several schools in special measures.

3. I have asked the class to watch 'wonder of the universe' this evening since the scientist brian cox will appear on it.

4. we are hoping that the school will appear in 'the yorkshire post' newspaper this evening.

5. my spanish class never do the homework i ask of them, but i know that some of them are watching 'narcos', which is better than nothing I suppose.

6. there are a few pupils in year 10 who are doing their work experience at boots.

7. some of our Eal students are performing below expectations.

8. since this is a roman catholic school, it is important that christmas is celebrated in the appropriate way.

9. the pupils always considered mr smith, the biology teacher, to be the most understanding.

10. i am happy that we don't need to teach latin in the school. trying to force the boys to engage with english and french is hard enough.

3.34 Capital practice answers

1. Pupil attainment is better in some parts of the UK than others.

2. In the London Borough of Lewisham, there are several schools in special measures.

3. I have asked the class to watch 'Wonder of the Universe' this evening since the scientist Brian Cox will appear on it.

4. We are hoping that the school will appear in 'The Yorkshire Post' newspaper this evening.

5. My Spanish class never do the homework I ask of them, but I know that some of them are watching 'Narcos', which is better than nothing I suppose.

6. There are a few pupils in year 10 who are doing their work experience at Boots.

7. Some of our EAL students are performing below expectations.

8. Since this is a Roman Catholic school, it is important that Christmas is celebrated in the appropriate way.

9. The pupils always considered Mr Smith, the biology teacher, to be the most understanding.

10. I am happy that we don't need to teach Latin in the school. Trying to force the boys to engage with English and French is hard enough.

3.35 Capital Test tips

It is likely that there will be a capitalisation error or two in the test. Scan through the text at the start to check that all paragraphs and sentences start with capital letters and check that there aren't obvious missing capital letters for people's names, book titles etc. Remember too that if you are inserting a full stop, you also need to amend the first word of the new sentence from lower case to a capital letter (and, as mentioned before, remember that this counts for two punctuation errors, not one).

3.36 Hyphens

The main purpose of a hyphen is to join two words together to form a compound word. The hyphen shows that the words joined together have a combined meaning and, on occasion, this can affect the overall meaning of a sentence.

Take a look at how the hyphen can change the meaning of the following two sentences:

I recently bought a little used bike.
I recently bought a little-used bike.

In the first example, the bike could be second-hand and small in size, whereas in the second example, because the words 'little' and 'used' have been linked together, we know that the sentence refers to a bike that has not been used very much (and this makes much more sense).

Although hyphen use can be quite complicated, missing hyphens should be relatively easy to spot in the QTS test because in the test, the word that requires the hyphen will be written as one word rather than two. For example, it might not be very obvious to you that the words 'little used' require a hyphen, but when it is written as 'littleused', which may look rather odd to you, hopefully you will quickly spot the problem.

Hyphens are most commonly used in compound adjectives (describing words), so be on the lookout in the QTS test for two adjectives which have been combined to form one word.

In the below examples, you should spot the missing hyphens quite easily because there are words which clearly need to be separated. Some of the words require more than one hyphen as well, although it is unlikely that in the test you will be required to add more than one hyphen in any compound word.

3.37 Hyphen practice questions

1. George is the fairhaired boy who sits at the back of the class.

2. The school banned all drinks from the canteen that were not sugarfree.

3. We have a custombuilt ICT suite on the new school site.

4. I always find George to be a very badtempered child.

5. If you opt for an apprenticeship, you are going to receive an abundance of onthejob training.

6. This new NQT is far too selfassured for my liking!

7. The content of this lesson is far too demanding for twelveyearold boys

8. Please read the uptodate guidance on how to move files from your laptop to the OneDrive.

9. The new building will be equipped with stateoftheart facilities.

10. This is not a oneoff incident: Jayden has displayed similar behaviour throughout the entire year.

3.38 Hyphen practice answers

1. George is the fair-haired boy who sits at the back of the class.

2. The school banned all drinks from the canteen that were not sugar-free.

3. We have a custom-built ICT suite on the new school site.

4. I always find George to be a very bad-tempered child.

5. If you opt for an apprenticeship, you are going to receive an abundance of on-the-job training.

6. This new NQT is far too self-assured for my liking!

7. The content of this lesson is far too demanding for twelve-year-old boys.

8. Please read the up-to-date guidance on how to move files from your laptop to the OneDrive.

9. The new building will be equipped with state-of-the-art facilities.

10. This is not a one-off incident: Jayden has displayed similar behaviour throughout the entire year.

3.39   Hyphen Test tips

There is a possibility that you will need to insert a hyphen in the punctuation text, but it is not a common feature of every test, and it is unlikely that you would need to add more than one.   If you are struggling to find all 15 punctuation omissions, it could be that you have not spotted a missing hyphen somewhere.   Go through the text again, looking for any large words that look unusual because they are a compound of two or more smaller words.

3.40   New paragraphs

Paragraphs break up a longer text into smaller and more manageable pieces. A paragraph is a distinct section of the text with a single theme or idea.

Let's take a look at a sample text:

Pastoral Support Managers are at the centre of all pastoral care within the school and should be the first point of contact for students and parents. They will deal with initial concerns or queries and investigate any incidents before referring matters to the appropriate House or Pastoral Leader. They will also liaise with individual subject staff and Curriculum Leaders to resolve any issues or concerns. In a minority of cases, they will also refer matters to the Deputy Head or other members of Senior Staff.   House Leaders are responsible for establishing and promoting the positive day to day behaviour of students and for ensuring that each individual student makes a positive contribution to all aspects of school life; House Leaders promote engagement, participation, contribution and achievement and are responsible for maintaining the school's accepted standards at all times. Pastoral Leaders are responsible for supporting the progress and learning of all students and work specifically with the students who present any long-term educational or disciplinary concerns. In addition, the Pastoral Leaders monitor a wide range of indicators relating to students in their year group(s) including; attendance, punctuality, positive conduct, negative conduct, detentions, rewards and sanctions. Pastoral Leaders lead the tutor teams and uphold all school expectations.

The above piece of text is noticeably long, so long in fact that it is not appealing to a potential reader (did you even try reading it?), so this is a clear sign that there is poor paragraphing.

If we investigate this text, it begins by talking about the role and responsibilities of Pastoral Support Managers and then, on the 7th line, it starts talking about the roles and responsibilities of House Leaders. Since this is a change of theme, this should be a new paragraph. The same applies in the 11th line where the theme switches again from House Leaders to Pastoral Leaders, so this would also require a new paragraph:

Pastoral Support Managers are at the centre of all pastoral care within the school and should be the first point of contact for students and parents. They will deal with initial concerns or queries and investigate any incidents before referring matters to the appropriate House or Pastoral Leader. They will also liaise with individual subject staff and Curriculum Leaders to resolve any issues or concerns. In a minority of cases, they will also refer matters to the Deputy Head or other members of Senior Staff.

House Leaders are responsible for establishing and promoting the positive day to day behaviour of students and for ensuring that each individual student makes a positive contribution to all aspects of school life; House Leaders promote engagement, participation, contribution and achievement and are responsible for maintaining the school's accepted standards at all times.

Pastoral Leaders are responsible for supporting the progress and learning of all students and work specifically with the students who present any long-term educational or disciplinary concerns. In addition, the Pastoral Leaders monitor a wide range of indicators relating to students in their year group(s) including; attendance, punctuality, positive conduct, negative conduct, detentions, rewards and sanctions. Pastoral Leaders lead the tutor teams and uphold all school expectations.

By paragraphing in this way, the text is much more visually appealing to the reader, and reading the entire text now doesn't seem such an arduous task.

3.41   New Paragraphs Test tips

In the QTS text, take a look at the length of the whole text. If there is a lot of text together, this is probably a sign that more paragraphing is required. Not every test will require you to create new paragraphs but, if it does, it is highly unlikely that you will need to use the // symbol more than once.

3.42 Strategy

It is quite possible that, having read and understood the above (and answered all the practice questions!), you now feel confident to tackle the punctuation text without any further guidance. However, if you would like a scaffolded general strategy to ensure you get as close to full marks in this section as possible, then I would propose the following 3 stage strategy:

Stage 1

In stage 1, what I would propose is to scan through the text looking for the most obvious punctuation omissions. Look for full stops, brackets, speech marks, inverted commas and capitals. Perhaps a daft phrase such as "Fluffy Bears Steal Ice Creams" might be a useful (albeit daft!) sentence to help you remember what to look out for in stage 1.

Fluffy: F = full stops. Focus on the easy ones! Is there a full stop at the end of the text / at the end of each paragraph / at the end of each section?

Bears: B = brackets. Brackets come in pairs. Are there any missing opening brackets or closing brackets?

Steal: S = speech marks. Speech marks come in pairs. Are there any missing opening speech marks or closing speech marks?

Ice: I = inverted commas. Inverted commas come in pairs. Is there an opening or closing inverted comma missing?

Creams: C = capitals. Is the first word of each paragraph and each sentence capitalised? Are there any proper nouns missing capital letters (names of people, places, books, films etc.).

At the end of stage 1, you have hopefully picked up a few marks without having had to really exert yourself. Add up the punctuation changes you have made and work out how many more you have left to find. In stage 1, you have not really had to engage with the text and understand what it is about, you were simply looking for glaring punctuation errors.

Stage 2

Now that you know how many punctuation omissions you have left to find, you are going to have to read the text in a bit more detail and engage with what it is trying to convey. Stage 2 is all about lists, commas, full stops and question marks.

It is quite possible that, while you are reading the text, there are certain phrases that don't make sense. You might have to reread some lines to try and make sense of what the author is trying to say. If you are struggling to understand certain parts of the text, then this is a clue that there is a punctuation problem. It could be that you are misreading the text because a full stop has been left out, meaning you are reading two sentences as if they were one, or maybe parts of the text don't make sense unless you pause at a certain point. So, in this stage, look for missing full stops and obvious commas. Remember, you use a comma for a quick pause for breath, and a full stop for a complete break. Do not go comma crazy! Simply add the ones you are certain of at this stage and pick up any missing ones in the final stage.

In stage 2, look for lists as well. If you find a list, is it introduced by a colon? Is each item separated by a comma or semicolon? You shouldn't need to worry about whether to use a semicolon or comma as it should be obvious from the list: other items in the list will be separated by semicolons or commas, so simply continue the pattern.

Are there questions in the text which do not have a question mark at the end?

Again, tally up the new total of punctuation alterations and work out how many you still need to find.

Stage 3

Now that you have completed the very easy stage 1 and the slightly more complicated stage 2, hopefully you don't have too many more punctuation omissions left to find. At this stage, you might be starting to struggle to find the remainder, since the remaining omissions might be harder to spot.

Apostrophes – check for missing apostrophes. Are there contracted words with apostrophes missing (cant) or apostrophes missing where possession is indicated? Remember, do not be tempted to start adding apostrophes to plurals simply to boost your tally to the required 15!

Paragraphs – does the text look excessively long? Does any individual paragraph look excessively long? This could be an indication that a new paragraph needs to be created somewhere. Remember that a new paragraph is required when there is a change of theme.

Hyphens – if you are struggling to find the remaining punctuation omissions, then consider looking for individual words that should be hyphenated. Is there a word that looks a little odd? Is this word a combination of two words? If so, and you are running out of other feasible options, add a hyphen.

More commas – assuming you have not gone comma crazy in stage 2, then it is highly likely that the remaining punctuation marks are commas. Commas can be a matter of personal taste and style (which is why I recommended only putting in the obvious ones in stage 2), so go through the text looking for the most obvious places to position them. Remember that, in general, a comma can be justified if you were to pause when reading the text aloud. Look for pauses after introductory phrases, before and after words like 'however', 'in general', and before and after dependent clauses that add additional information, especially phrases starting with 'who' and 'which'.

3.43   Punctuation General tips

It may seem obvious, but do make sure that the punctuation you have spotted has actually been applied to the text. Don't assume that the apostrophe has appeared after you have clicked the apostrophe button, check that it is there, and check that it is in the position you intended as well!

When adding commas, make sure you put the comma in the correct place. Don't highlight a word and then just click the comma button, because this will automatically add a comma at the start of the word, whereas you will probably want to position the comma at the end of the word.

Make sure you make 15 alterations in total!

100

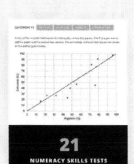
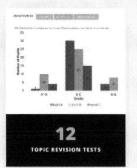
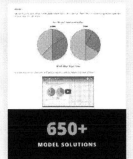
101

QTS LITERACY TUTOR
WWW.LITERACYSKILLSTEST.CO.UK

★★★★★ Based on hundreds of reviews on ★ Trustpilot

FREE ONLINE LITERACY SKILLS TEST
EXPERT 1 TO 1 TUITION WITH OUR QTS SPECIALISTS

—— WHAT QTS LITERACY TUTOR HAS TO OFFER ——

Spelling Practice   Punctuation Questions   Grammar Section   Comprehension Resources

Practice Tests   Expert Tutors   Correct Format   New Question Formats

Visit www.literacyskillstest.co.uk to take a Free Full Practice Test today.

10
LITERACY SKILLS TESTS

97%
LEARNER PASS RATE

490
TEST QUESTIONS

4.0 Grammar

- Questions: 3-4
- Marks: 10 - 12
- Percentage of paper: 20% - 26%
- Recommended time spent on this paper: 10 minutes
- What is considered a good mark for this section? 8 or above

The grammar section is a gap-fill exercise where you are presented with 3 texts (usually letters). In each text, there are between 3 - 4 questions, and for each question, you need to fill a gap in the text from one of the 3 - 4 options available. If English is your first language then, a lot of the time, some of the answers are reasonably obvious. If the correct answer is not obvious, then you may at least notice that there are some answers which are very obviously wrong, leaving you with fewer remaining options to guess from if required.

Below is a breakdown of the most common grammatical points that the test focuses on.

4.1 Grammatical point 1: inconsistency between subject and verb

Subjects and verbs have to agree with each other in terms of number. What this means is that a singular subject must have a singular verb and a plural subject must have a plural verb:

The cat is playing with the string. ('The cat' is singular so we need the singular form 'is' from the verb 'to be'.)

The cats are playing with the string. ('The cats' are plural so we need the plural form 'are' from the verb 'to be'.)

A lot of people mix up the verb forms 'was' and 'were', specifically using 'was' with a plural, which is incorrect:

There was a boy in the changing room. ('was' is singular because 'a boy' is singular)

There were two boys in the changing room. ('were' is plural because 'boys' is plural)

'There was two boys in the changing room' is completely incorrect and unacceptable.

Be careful when there are collective nouns (a class, team, group etc.). When a collective noun is used in the singular, then the verb is singular, even when the group contains more than one person:

35 hyperactive children are *difficult to manage.* (Plural verb because there is a plural subject)

15 girls were *left in the hall.* (Plural verb because there is a plural subject)

A class *of 35 hyperactive children* **is** *difficult to manage.* (Singular verb because 'a class' is singular.)

A group *of 15 girls* **was** *left in the hall.* (Singular verb because 'a group' is singular.)

When there is more than one subject, you need to use a plural verb, even if the item that precedes the verb is singular:

*A positive mental attitude and a dictionary **are** all you need in my French lessons!*

However, if the items are linked by the word 'or', then you would use the singular form of the verb:

*A positive mental attitude or a dictionary **is** all you need in my French lessons!*

When a sentence starts with each or every, the verb is singular:

*Every child **matters**.*

*Each person in this class **is** responsible for their learning.*

When there is an additional phrase or clause after the subject, the verb agreement can be hard to spot.

*The teachers who attended the meeting **were** bored.* (The verb must agree with 'teachers' which is plural. The verb does not agree with the singular word 'meeting'. Remember that it is the teachers that were bored, and not the meeting.)

*The politics of the school **were** horrific.* (The verb must agree with 'politics' which is plural. The verb does not agree with the singular word 'school'. Remember that it is the politics of the school that were horrific, not the school itself.)

Here is another example where there are potentially misleading options to choose from:

The headteacher, who is likely to be made redundant following allegations of unnecessarily excluding troublesome students, claims there has been no wrongdoing.

The headteacher, who is likely to be made redundant following allegations of unnecessarily excluding troublesome students, claim there has been no wrongdoing.

In a sentence like this, do not let a 'who' clause distract you from what the subject is. The subject is 'the headteacher' (singular) so the verb 'claims' must also be singular. Sometimes it is worth ignoring additional clauses, especially 'who' or 'which' statements, so that you aren't distracted from the main clause. In this example, it is not the students that are claiming, which is why the first and not the second example is correct.

Here is one final example:

I am particularly pleased by Gareth's attitude in science and maths which is very important as it shows he has taken on board what was discussed in our recent meeting.

I am particularly pleased by Gareth's attitude in science and maths which are very important as it shows he has taken on board what was discussed in our recent meeting.

If you don't give these questions the attention they deserve, you may think the first option is incorrect because the phrase '.....science and maths which is important' is not grammatically correct. You must comb through the text and work out what the subject of the verb is. What is important? Is it science and maths (plural) or is it Gareth's attitude (singular)? The final part of the sentence, 'as it shows....', tells us that it is Gareth's attitude that is very important in this sentence which is why the second example is correct.

It is very likely that there will be examples of subject and verb disagreement in your QTS test. Eliminate any examples where you see this!

4.2   Grammatical point 2: inconsistency with verb tenses

It is essential in the QTS test to ensure that you can recognise lack of consistency with verb tenses. It is acceptable to have different verb tenses in one sentence when the verbs refer to different periods of time.   For example:

John was on target for a grade 7 last year, but he is currently working at a grade 4.

In this sentence, we have used the past tense 'was' to refer to what happened last year followed by the present tense 'is' to refer to what is currently happening.

If a sentence refers only to past events, then the past tense should be used throughout. It would be incorrect to say:

Last week, Gareth sat the maths test and achieves 56%.

This entire sentence refers to events in the past, so the past tense needs to be continued throughout in order to maintain verb tense consistency.

As far as the past tense is concerned, note that in English, there are two past tenses.   One refers to a specific time in the past (the simple past tense: normally accompanied by a past tense time phrase such as 'yesterday', 'last week' etc.) and the other refers to an undefined time in the past (the past perfect: this tense will use the word 'have' or 'has').

Last year, I went to China.

Last year, I have gone to China.

In these examples, the second sentence is incorrect. When you refer to a specific time in the past ('last year' in this example), you use the simple past tense which is the past tense without the 'have' or 'has'.

If a sentence refers only to future events, then the future tense should generally be used throughout. It would be incorrect to say:

Next week, Simon will sit his maths GCSE and starts his part-time job the following Saturday.

This entire sentence refers to events in the future, so the future tense needs to be continued throughout in order to maintain verb tense consistency.

Verbs of hoping or looking forward can pose a problem as well. This is because you hope that something will happen in the future, or you look forward to something happening in the future. However, the actual act of hoping, or looking forward to something, normally occurs in the present, so a present tense is generally required.

I hope that I will succeed in my exams. (The succeeding is going to take place at some stage in the future, hence the future tense, but the hoping is happening in the present, hence the present tense. 'I will hope' would be incorrect in this example.)

I am looking forward to receiving my GCSE results and will be happy if I achieve a grade 5 in maths. (The being happy is going to take place at some stage in the future, hence the future tense, but the looking forward is happening in the present, hence the present tense. 'I will look forward' would be incorrect in this example. Note too that after 'if', English uses the present tense even though there is reference to a future action (this is different in other languages like French where it would be correct to use the future tense).)

There is a very high chance that you will see possible answers which contain verb tense inconsistencies, or answers which are inconsistent in tense to the question. These verb tense inconsistencies usually make the meaning unclear and confused, so are generally easy to spot. Make sure you read the options carefully and keep an eye out for any tense inconsistency.

4.3   Grammatical point 3: inconsistency in lists

When you see lists in the test, make sure that there is consistency in how each item is introduced.

This meeting is:

a) *an opportunity to raise important concerns about your upcoming appraisal and discussing how to set yourself measurable targets*

The above is a classic example of the type of incorrect option you could face. In this list, there are two key ideas being presented. The first is 'raising concerns' and the second is 'discussing targets'. However, both these items are presented differently in the list. What you have to do is analyse the sentence, and work out where in the sentence these two ideas attach to. In this example, the phrase 'this meeting is an opportunity to' is the phrase that both items are attached to. The first example 'raise important concerns' fits perfectly after 'an opportunity to', but the phrase 'discussing' simply does not fit after 'an opportunity to'. Therefore this answer can be eliminated and you should search for an answer where both list items do make sense after the phrase 'an opportunity to'. In this example, the correct answer would be:

This meeting is:

a) *an opportunity to **raise** important concerns about your upcoming appraisal and **discuss** how to set yourself measurable targets*

'Raise' and 'discuss' match in a grammatical sense, in a way that 'raise' and 'discussing' do not.

Here is another example:

Prior to the deadline of January 15, all year 10 boys are expected to:

a) *write an up-to-date CV; complete the work experience questionnaire; you should send in a scanned copy of your passport; read the Grange Hill Work Experience Handbook.*

Like the previous example, the items in this list are inconsistent. 'Write', 'complete' and 'read' are all grammatically similar verb forms which fit after the opening statement and after the word 'to'. However, 'you should send' does not match this consistency and when it is attached to this opening statement will read:

Prior to the deadline of January 15, all year 10 boys are expected to you should send in a scanned copy of your passport.

This clearly makes no sense whatsoever so can be eliminated. The correct option would read:

110

Prior to the deadline of January 15, all year 10 boys are expected to:

a) **write** *an up-to-date CV;* **complete** *the work experience questionnaire;* **send** *in a scanned copy of your passport;* **read** *the Grange Hill Work Experience Handbook.*

In this example, the four verb forms are consistent which means that the sentence now makes sense.

4.4   Grammatical point 4: misuse of should have / could have / would have / may have / might have

This is an extremely common error among English native speakers! So many people write 'should **of**' rather than 'should **have**', 'could **of**' instead of 'could **have**' and 'would **of**' instead of 'would **have**'. The reason for this common error is because we often use the contracted form 'should've' when we speak, and the shortening of the 'have' to ' 've ' sounds very much like the word 'of'. (Please note that, although the pronunciation of the ' 've ' in 'would've' might sound similar to 'of', it is not the exact pronunciation of the word 'of', whatever part of the English speaking world you come from! It should be said as more of an 'uv' sound than an 'ov' sound!)

In the test, discard every option where there is a 'should of', 'may of', 'could of' etc. These are all grammatically incorrect!

In some texts, you may see two separate and grammatically correct options, where the only difference is a difference in meaning because one sentence contains 'should have' and the other contains 'could have'.

'Could have' means that something was possible at some point in the past, but it did not happen:

Steve could have stopped the boy from falling.

In this sentence, it was possible for Steve to stop the boy from falling, but he didn't (for whatever reason).

'Should have' means that something did not happen, but we wish it had happened.

Mary should have called the police.

Mary did not call the police, and this was clearly a mistake or oversight on her part.

4.5   Grammatical point 5: and I / and me / and myself

There is a lot of confusion about whether you should use 'me' or 'I' in a sentence, but this confusion can easily be eliminated.

John and I went to the cinema.

John and me went to the cinema.

Which of the above is correct? The simplest way to check is to imagine how you would write this sentence if John hadn't gone to the cinema and the speaker had gone on their own. The sentences would read:

I went to the cinema.

Me went to the cinema.

Because it is grammatically correct to say 'I went to the cinema' and not 'me went to the cinema', that is why you would write 'John and I' and not 'John and me'.

This problem is less obvious when the person speaking is the object of the sentence:

Sue came to the cinema with John and I.

Sue came to the cinema with John and me.

Again, like the previous example, what would you write if Sue had gone to the cinema with the speaker and there was no John? The sentences would then read:

Sue came to the cinema with I.

Sue came to the cinema with me.

Because it is grammatically correct to say 'with me' and not 'with I', that is why you would have to write 'John and me' and not 'John and I' in this example.

As far as 'myself' is concerned, you cannot use it as a subject or object. These following sentences are not correct:

Steve and myself were interrogated by the headteacher.

Simon played football with Gary and myself.

These sentences should read:

Steve and I were interrogated by the headteacher.

Simon played football with Gary and me.

In the test, if you see an option with a 'myself' in it, it is highly likely that it can be discarded immediately.

4.6 Grammatical point 6: misuse of relative pronouns (who, whom and which)

'Who' and 'whom' are used to refer to people, not things, and the misuse of 'who' and 'whom' is very common. A lot of people use 'who' instead of 'whom', but this mistake is rarely noticed; it is almost as if this is an acceptable mistake to make. 'The boy who I saw....' is not grammatically correct English. It should be 'The boy whom I saw....'. (You might even think that the sentence sounds better with 'who' rather than 'whom', even though it is technically incorrect!)

Some people misuse the word 'whom' by using it when they should simply say 'who', and this is a mistake which is far more obvious. Certain people, if they are in a formal situation, or if they are wishing to give the impression of being more intelligent or educated, use 'whom' when they would usually say 'who'. Unfortunately, while the person may be trying to show off how educated they are by using 'whom' and not 'who', they might in fact be doing the opposite since they are making a glaring grammatical error.

Here is an example of 'whom' being incorrectly used:

We have decided to exclude your son, whom is not responding to our interventions, for three weeks.

The sentence should read:

We have decided to exclude your son, who is not responding to our interventions, for three weeks.

Let's make this explanation as simple as possible. If you are facing the choice between 'who' and 'whom', simply look at the next word in the

114

sentence. If the word after 'who' or 'whom' is a verb, then use 'who'. If the word after 'who' or 'whom' is a new subject (another person), then use 'who'.

This is the boy whom we saw. ('Whom' because it is not followed immediately by a verb, but by a new subject 'we'.)

This is the boy who is top of the class. ('Who' because it is followed immediately by a verb.)

'Which' is used for objects and things, never for people:

The book, which is on the table, is the one the boy would like to read.

'What' should never be used in this context. Sentences of the type 'The boy what came to school', 'The book what is on the table' are ugly and wrong!

4.7   Grammatical point 7: these kinds / types / sorts of

You may be faced in the test with a set of options like this:

- a.   *these kinds of opportunity*
- b.   *this kinds of opportunity*
- c.   *these kind of opportunities*
- d.   *these kinds of opportunities*

If the noun being used is singular, then it should be preceded by 'this kind (singular) / sort (singular) / type (singular) of':

*This **kind** of **scheme***

*This **type** of **assessment***

*This **sort** of **feedback***

If the noun being used is plural, then it should be preceded by 'these kinds (plural) / sorts (plural) / types (plural) of':

*These **kinds** of **schemes***

*These **types** of **assessments***

*These **sorts** of **tests***

The same applies if the word being used is 'that' or those': 'that type of' followed by a singular noun and 'those types of' followed by a plural noun.

I would argue that it is possible to say 'these types of scheme' as well as 'these types of schemes' and that there is a subtle difference in meaning between the two, but as far as the test is concerned, rule out 'these types of' followed by a singular noun in favour of 'these types of' followed by a plural noun. Do be aware that there are many resources online and in other literacy books that have incorrectly explained this rule, even giving examples of grammatically incorrect sentences!

4.8   Grammatical point 8: use of tautologies (redundant / unnecessary language)

The test advice states that in written English, meaning should be expressed 'clearly and concisely', and sometimes less is more. Redundant language refers to information that is expressed more than once in a sentence. In the test, you may see examples of redundant language in the options, and these options should be avoided. Here are some examples of tautologies:

*The track and field events will commence at the **following** times **below**.* ('Following' or ' below', but not both.)

The reason for this is because he has failed his mock test. ('Because' and 'the reason for this' are similar in meaning so this sentence can be written as 'The reason for this is that he has failed his mock test' or 'This is because he has failed his mock test'.)

That is a huge over-exaggeration. (An 'exaggeration' already indicates that it is over the top)

The meeting took place at 9am in the morning.

Let's write a short summary of the first chapter.

An added bonus.

A new innovation.

An ATM machine (the 'M' of 'ATM' already stands for 'machine')

4.9 Grammatical point 9: choosing the incorrect homophone

Homophones are a problem because they are words which are different in meaning and in spelling, but which have the same pronunciation (hear/here, bear/bare, know/no, mail/male, meat/meet, right/write, wear/where etc.). Here are some of the common ones which could cause problems in the test:

Affect and effect

'Affect' is usually a verb meaning to make a difference to or to influence. *The teacher can affect the outcomes of his students by giving better feedback on their assessments.*

Because 'affect' is a verb, it can exist in other verb forms such as 'affecting' and 'affected'. ('Affect' is also a noun, but you are unlikely to see it as a noun in the test.)

'Effect' is usually a noun. Its definition is a result or consequence of an action. *The number of supply teachers in our school is definitely having an effect on the students.*

'Effect' can be a verb when it means to cause something to happen or to bring about. *The head teacher effected many changes to the behaviour policy.*

'Effective', which comes from the noun 'effect', is an adjective which means that something is producing results.

'Affective' is an adjective which means relating to moods and feelings. It is a word used in the field of psychology, so unlikely to appear in the test, although it could be used in an incorrect answer option.

In the test, assume that if it is a noun, the spelling is 'effect' and if it is a verb, it is 'affect'.

Practice and practise

'Practice' is a noun. *Football practice is on Wednesdays at 4.30pm.*

'Practise' is a verb. *You need to practise your times tables in order to perform well in the mental arithmetic section of the QTS maths test.*

Advice and advise

'Advice' is a noun. *He gave me some excellent advice.*

'Advise' is a verb. *The teacher advised me to sit the foundation tier.*

Its and it's

' It's ' only requires the apostrophe when it means 'it is'. Only use 'its' when the meaning is 'belonging to it'.

It's (it is) *a sunny day today.*

The bag and its contents (the contents of it).

If you see the word ' it's ' as one of the grammar options, ask yourself if it would make sense if the word was replaced by 'it is'. If the sentence does not make sense when you replaced ' it's ' with 'it is', then this is an option that should be immediately discarded. The word ' its' ' does not exist in English, so any examples containing this incorrect spelling should also be eliminated.

There / Their / They're

'There' is used to indicate a place. 'There' is the opposite of 'here', so takes on a similar spelling (you wouldn't write 'heir' or ' hey're ', would you?).

I asked you to sit over there.

It is also used with the verb 'to be' in various tenses for the phrases 'there is', 'there are', 'there were', 'there would be' etc.

'Their' is used to indicate possession and will always be followed by a noun (an object or thing).

Their behaviour is slowly starting to improve.

' They're ' is a contraction (squeezing together) of the words 'they' and 'are'. It is not a contraction of the words 'there are'.

They're going to do a dress rehearsal of 'Macbeth' to the year 7s this afternoon.

If you are not sure which of the three to use, ask yourself whether it would make sense to replace the their / there / they're with the words 'they are'. If the answer is yes, then ' they're ' is the correct option. If the answer is no, then at least you have eliminated ' they're ' as an option and now have to decide between 'there' and 'their'. Now ask yourself if possession is indicated, or check to see if the following word is a noun. If the answer is yes, then use 'their', otherwise use 'there'.

Two / Too / To

'Two' is a number.

'Too' means 'also', 'in addition' or 'excessively'.

'To' is a preposition and should be used when you aren't referring to the number two or a word with the meaning of 'also' or 'excessively'.

Who's / Whose

Do not confuse ' who's ' which is a contracted form for 'who is' with 'whose' (belonging to whom). 'Whose' will normally be followed by a noun (an object or thing) or the word 'is' or 'are' when used as a question word. If you can replace ' who's ' or 'whose' with the words 'who is', then you know that ' who's ' is correct.

Simon is the boy who's (who is) at risk of permanent exclusion.

Simon is the boy whose parents are coming to see the music teacher. ('Who is' does not make sense in this example.)

Whose is this book? ('Who is' does not make sense in this example.)

Your and you're

This is another extremely high-frequency error in English, with many people using 'your' when they should write ' you're '. ' You're ' is a contracted form for 'you are'. 'Your' is a possessive adjective and will be followed by a noun. If you can replace ' you're ' or 'your' with the words 'you are', then you know that ' you're ' is correct.

Been / Being

This is a far less common error since these words are not homophones, but still one that can catch a few people out. 'Been' is the past participle of the verb 'to be' and, as such, can only be used with the words 'have', 'has' or 'had' before it. You cannot put these words in front of the word 'being'.

The boy's attitude in the physics lesson had been poor. (It has to be 'been' and not 'being' since there is a 'had' before it.)

4.10   Grammatical point 10: clumsy language

There will be answer options available to you in the test which can be eliminated simply because they do not make sense. These should be relatively easy to spot if you read the answer options with care. Remember that as well as selecting a grammatically correct answer, answers should make sense within the context and should be consistent in style and tone.

You may see answer options where a wrong word has been inserted which is contradictory to the points being made.

John has been making sound progress in maths, and has shown in a recent test that algebra is one of his strong points. For instance, there were some questions on trigonometry which he was unable to answer so this is a topic which will require further revision.

The problem with this example is the words 'for instance'. 'For instance' would make sense if the teacher was going to produce evidence to support the previous statement about John being good at algebra. In the second sentence, the teacher has mentioned some things which John was unable to do, so the second sentence deals with John's maths weaknesses whereas sentence one mentioned his strengths, so there is a contrast between these two sentences, so 'for instance' is not suitable. 'However' or 'On the other hand' would be more appropriate options.

If you are struggling to decipher a given option, then this could be because the statement is non-sensical. If it doesn't make sense, discard it! With answer options of this type, take your time, eliminating the ones which you know are wrong. If it is not obvious what is wrong, then compare the differences from one answer to the next, asking yourself what it is that makes one answer better or worse than the previous one. Here is an example:

a) *Any teacher organising a trip that requires the use of public transport should ensure that there is a ratio of 1 adult with DBS clearance for every 6 students wearing lanyards with emergency contact details, and that all students are equipped with a topped-up travel card.*

b) *Any teacher organising a trip that requires the use of public transport should ensure that there is a ratio of 1 adult with DBS clearance for every*

6 students, that all students are equipped and wearing topped-up travel card and lanyards with emergency contact details.

c) *Any teacher organising a trip that requires the use of public transport should ensure that there is a ratio of 1 adult with DBS clearance for every 6 students, that all students are equipped with a topped-up travel card and that they are all wearing lanyards with emergency contact details.*

d) *Any teacher organising a trip that requires the use of public transport should ensure that there is a ratio of 1 adult for every 6 students with DBS clearance, that all students are equipped with a topped-up travel card and that they are all wearing lanyards with emergency contact details.*

If you were confronted with the above in the test, you might have the following thought process:

When you read answer A, you are not immediately convinced it is a non-sensical answer, but there are one or two things that make you frown while you try to decipher it (frowning is usually a sign that there is a problem). The answer definitely makes sense up to the word 'students' and perhaps makes sense even as far as the word 'lanyards' or 'details'. However, there seems to be a problem with the final phrase as you can't seem to connect the '...and that' sentence to an earlier part of the text. You are not sure about this one. You feel that it is probably not correct, but you won't eliminate it just yet to be on the safe side.

When you read answer B, again, it reads well up to '6 students' but then there are some discrepancies. The answer mentions being 'equipped', but what with? Although it is grammatically correct just to say that students should be 'equipped', surely there should be some guidance or some description as to what being 'equipped' constitutes. It also mentions wearing a travel card which seems rather bizarre. From a grammar and punctuation point of view, it doesn't appear to make sense either as there is an issue with the 'that' clauses. There are only two 'that' clauses, the second of which comes after a comma. Either this second (and final) 'that' clause should come after an 'and' or a third 'that' clause should be added.

Answer C seems to read well and there is consistency with the use of the 'that' statements. This is definitely the best answer so far, and if you compare this to option A, then you feel that answer C is far more likely at this stage.

Answer D seems very similar to statement C. The only difference is the positioning of the words 'with DBS clearance'. In this answer, it reads that it is the students who require the DBS checks and not the teachers, so on this basis, you decide that answer C must be the correct answer.

You may see answer options where the tone of the language has changed. If the text is a letter from a headteacher to parents, it is likely to have a formal and professional tone and is unlikely to contain the phrase 'the behaviour of your son is driving me bonkers, and if it doesn't improve, I'm going to have him chucked out.' If you have eliminated a couple of the options and are not sure which of the remaining two to choose from, look at the tone or look at the length (generally speaking, shorter options are more likely to be more correct than the longer ones, provided they make sense).

Here are a few other grammar points which are worthy of your consideration and could conceivably feature in the test.

Fewer and less

Understanding when to use 'fewer' or 'less' comes down to appreciating whether a word is countable or not countable. Generally, people are more likely to use 'less' when they should say 'fewer', rather than the other way around.

There were fewer boys in the detention than usual. Here we use 'fewer' because you can count boys (one boy, two boys etc.)

There was less participation in the classroom than normal. (Here we use 'less' because you can't count participation (one participation, two participations etc. does not make sense)

Comparatives (more / less ... than) and superlatives (the most / the least)

The problem with comparatives and superlatives is that in English, there are two different ways to form them.

We can form a comparative either by putting the word 'more' or 'less' in front of the adjective, and the word 'than' after the adjective. For certain adjectives (generally ones which are short with one syllable), we simply add '-er' to the adjective.

Simon is more intelligent than Peter. (You would not say *'Simon is intelligenter than Peter.'*)

Simon is shorter than Peter. (You would not say *'Simon is more short than Peter.'*)

A lot of English-speaking people make the mistake of combining the above two rules and end up producing utterances such as:

Simon is more shorter than Peter.

This is completely incorrect! Depending on the adjective you are using, you either use the word 'more' or 'less', or you add the '-er' ending to the adjective.

We can form a superlative either by putting the words 'the most' or 'the least' in front of the adjective. For certain adjectives (generally ones which are short with one syllable), we put the word 'the' before the adjective and add '-est' to the adjective.

Simon is the most intelligent in the class.

Simon is the shortest in the class.

A lot of English-speaking people make the mistake of combining the above two rules and end up producing utterances such as:

Simon is the most shortest in the class.

Again, this is completely incorrect! Depending on the adjective you are using, you either use the words 'the most' or 'the least' with the adjective in its usual form, or you use the word 'the' with an adjective with '-est' at the end.

4.11   Apostrophes

Some options may have incorrect use of apostrophes (see correct apostrophe use in the punctuation chapter). It is possible that you will encounter plurals which have apostrophes or plural words that have apostrophes in the wrong place.

5.0   Reading comprehension

- Questions: 3-5 based on one text
- Marks: 10-12
- Percentage of paper: 20% - 26%
- Recommended time spent on this paper: 20 - 25 minutes
- What is considered a good mark for this section? 7-9 or above

The reading comprehension section of the QTS test is, without doubt, the hardest part, and is also quite difficult to prepare for. It is essential that you complete the spelling, punctuation and grammar sections quickly and efficiently in order to leave yourself with plenty of time to tackle the reading comprehension, which is also the most time-consuming part of the test.

Even if you are an avid reader, I imagine that it is unlikely that you would choose to read for pleasure the types of text they select for the test, as the texts can be quite heavy-going and difficult to understand. It is very easy to lose concentration while reading articles of this nature, especially when you are reading on screen rather than on paper, as well as reading it under a certain degree of pressure, so it is vital that you give the text your best attention. If you are tired when you take the test, you may find the text especially difficult to focus on, so do make sure that you give yourself the best chance of doing your best by ensuring you have had a good night's rest prior to the test and perhaps have a strong coffee before you enter the test centre!

When you start the reading comprehension text, read the text from start to finish in order to obtain a general gist of what the passage is about. Do not worry about the questions at this stage. If you jump in to the questions too early, skimming and scanning the text for answers, you are definitely not going to perform well. Before tackling the questions, you need to make sure you have read and, more importantly, fully understood the text.

It is quite possible that upon reading the text for the first time, you may not have understood much, but this is completely normal. Read the text again, so that the text starts to make a bit more sense. Remember that reading the text does not simply mean reading the individual words, it means reading and, at the same time, making sense of each sentence and each paragraph, so that as you are reading, you are generating an overall understanding of the passage. With texts of this nature, you will need to read much more slowly and carefully than usual. This is 'deep reading', a process which is under threat as we move into digital-based modes of reading. During your second reading, reread any paragraph that you have not fully understood, not moving on to the next paragraph until you have a clear idea about what you have just read. Once you have read and understood the first few paragraphs, this should set you up well to make better progress with your comprehension of the remainder of the text.

It may take you a good five to ten minutes to read and reread the text before you fully understand it, but this is definitely time well spent. See the time you spend preparing as an investment, because if you know the text well, then there is a good chance that you will be able to answer the questions much more efficiently. You may find that you are able to answer some of the questions without even having to refer back to the text (although I would always suggest checking the text to be on the safe side). Good knowledge of the text will also mean that you can locate the necessary paragraph quickly and efficiently when you are trying to locate evidence for an answer.

In the same way that you will have read the text with attention and care, do the same with the questions. Missing a key word in a question (or in one of the answer options), could have disastrous consequences. You should also read every answer option before choosing your response. If you think the first answer option is the correct one, do not simply select it without even considering the others (other answer options may be more relevant, or the option you thought was correct could be a distractor). Do not use your own prior knowledge to answer questions. All answers options are evidenced in the text, so you do not need to use your own opinion, even if you are convinced that your opinion is better than that of the author!

If there is a certain question that you are struggling with in the text, don't waste too much time on it. Simply move on and come back to it later. It could be that you didn't understand the question because you have not yet gained a full understanding of the text. The question you are struggling with might become less complicated once you have tackled subsequent questions, as the other questions might help unlock extra information which you have missed.

There are certain question types that are likely to appear in the text which I have outlined below. You will not see all of these question types in your test, perhaps only three or four of them.

5.1 <u>Selecting an appropriate title, heading, or sub-heading</u>

You may be asked to choose an appropriate title for the text, or for a given paragraph, from a list of options. In order to select the best heading option, you need to consider the text as a whole. What is the main point of the article? A headline often provides the answer to the key points of the article. For example, the newspaper headline 'Strong universities lessen social tensions' tells us everything we need to know about the article that follows, grabbing our attention and drawing us in (provided that we are interested in education and social issues of course). If you are asked to select a sub-heading for a section or paragraph, then you need to consider what the main points of that section or paragraph only are, rather than the entire text.

Example question (2 marks): select two most appropriate titles for this article:

- Debt collectors employed in state schools
- Cost of school trips spiralling out of control
- Parents asked to cover funding shortfall
- School trips cancelled due to Brexit
- Free education disappearing before our eyes
- Equality in state sector schools at last
- Ofsted says parents to pay for compulsory text books
- Schools requesting parental contributions judged 'outstanding'

5.2   <u>Selecting the audience type for such an article</u>

For this type of question you have to choose the group of people that you think would be most interested and least interested in the article from a list of potential audience types. Choices could include: headteachers, heads of faculty, Ofsted inspectors, primary school teachers, parents, teachers of a particular subject, or government ministers. This is probably one of the easier question types in theory, although don't rush in with an answer without considering the text as a whole. Just because the headline of the article is 'IT misuse soaring in schools' does not mean that the article is aimed specifically at teachers of IT; the article may be written in a way that means that this is an issue which headteachers, or perhaps teachers in general, should be addressing.

Example question (2 marks): the following groups might all be potential audiences or readers of the article, although some of them would find it more useful than others. Which group would find it the most relevant and which group would find it the least relevant?

- Primary school teachers
- Teachers that organise overseas trips
- Ofsted inspectors
- Parents of school children
- Pastoral staff
- Heads of year
- Headteachers
- Debt collecting agencies

5.3 <u>Selecting a phrase which is closest in meaning to a given phrase from the text</u>

You may be faced with a couple of questions of this type in the text, and these can be quite difficult. Naturally, the phrases you will face are the more complicated phrases in the text containing challenging vocabulary, for example 'the concept of globalisation is stoking social tensions'. However, they do assist you by telling you which paragraph the phrase can be found in, so reread the whole paragraph so that you can see the phrase in an appropriate context. With any luck, however, you may already understand the phrase and not need to refer to the text, simply reading through the answer options until you find the option that you know has the same or similar meaning to the given phrase.

Example question (2 marks): Select the most appropriate alternative for each phrase as it appears in the context of the passage.

'their proliferation is hard to ignore' (paragraph 3) is closest in meaning to:

- a) it is easy to see that they are becoming more popular
- b) we can't pretend to not see how important they are
- c) it is difficult to not notice how common they are
- d) ignoring is difficult due to their decrease

5.4 Selecting statements that accurately convey information in the text

You may be presented with a list of eight statements, from which you have to select four which are true, based on the information in the text. If you have read and understood the text well, then you should be able to quickly select, or exclude, certain options. For any options you are not sure about, you will need to reread the text from start to finish (or, at the very least, the relevant section of the text) in order to confirm if the statement is true or false. If you are unsure about every answer option, then you will potentially need to comb through the text multiple times. Since this could be quite a time-consuming activity, it might be best to abandon this question for now, and move on before returning later, time permitting.

Example question (4 marks): select the four statements that are true:

a) Everybody understands the term 'information literacy'

b) With poor information literacy skills, students may not be able to recognise whether the information they are reading can be trusted or not

c) Information literacy is probably one of the most relevant subjects taught in schools

d) Information literacy helps to assist boys appreciate the relevance of French

e) A good way to promote information literacy is to allow students to use it in an area that interests them

f) Promoting information literacy might result in fewer students submitting plagiarised work

g) Independent learning is rarely underpinned by information

h) The first thing educators need to do is convince people of the need for information before convincing them of the need for information literacy

5.5   Selecting the main points of the text or part of text

This is a very similar question type to selecting statements that accurately convey information, described above.   However, focus on what the main points are, ignoring any statements which may be true, but which are not really pivotal to the text as a whole.

5.6   Completing a list

If the text contains a list of bullet points, you may be asked to complete a list of similar bullet points from a set of options. You need to select the options which are as close as possible in meaning to the original bullet point items in the text. Simply compare the answer options to the bullet points in the list and select the ones which you believe are the same in meaning.

Example question (4 marks): Select the four most appropriate statements to complete the bulleted list which appears in the passage:

In introducing IL (Information Literacy) to students emphasise:

-

- that it helps us in our efforts to retrain in order to ensure continued employability in a changing workplace

-

-

-

a) that it is imperative for us to gain a sound understanding of what is going on in the world

b) that it can help us in our quest to become more educated

c) that there is more to computers than social media

d) that it is imperative to be fluent with everyday packages that are used in business

e) how crucial it is in order for us to make good choices in everyday situations and when making purchases

f) how important it is to improve our general literacy

g) that is enables us to learn more about the things which appeal to us

h) that it enable us to stay on top of current affairs

5.7   Selecting categories for statements

For this question type, you will be given three or four statements which need to be matched to a single word answer or category. This is a drag and drop activity where there are the same number of answers as questions, so is theoretically even easier than a multiple-choice question since every answer option has to be used. You may have four statements which you need to match up to, for example, different education provider types (e.g. secondary schools, primary schools, pupil referral units and universities) so you simply have to decide which of the education providers fits the statement best, again, based on the evidence provided in the text. Additionally, if there are four questions, and you have already worked out three of them and are convinced that they are correct, then the fourth one should automatically be correct by default (although worth checking that this final answer makes sense too and, if it doesn't, that tells you that one of your previous answers is wrong as well).

Example question (3 marks): read the following questions and select which refer to:

- illegality
- irrationality
- procedural impropriety

1. Did the headteacher and / or governing body act outside the scope of their legal powers in taking the decision to exclude?
2. Did the governing board rely on irrelevant points, fail to take account of all relevant points or make a decision so unreasonable that no governing board acting reasonably in such circumstances could have made it?
3. Was the process of exclusion and the governing body's consideration so unfair or flawed that justice was clearly not done?

5.8   Deciding the extent to which a statement is supported by the text if at all

In the test, you will be given some statements and you need to decide if the statement is:

a) **supported** by the text **(S)**

b) **implied** in the text **(I)**

c) **not evidenced** in the text **(NE)**

d) **implicitly contradicted** in the text **(IC)**

e) **explicitly contradicted** in the text **(EC)**

This is definitely one of the harder set of test questions which can sometimes lead to some ambiguous and debatable answers.

If you can point to evidence in the text that supports the statement, then you should choose the 'supported' option. If you can't point to evidence in the text that supports the statement but, reading between the lines, you believe it to be true, then select the 'implied' option.

You will use the 'no evidence' choice if the statement is not supported, implied or contradicted in the text, so if you are struggling with a particular question and feel that guessing is the only option, then the 'no evidence' option might be the most sensible.

If you can point to evidence in the text that disagrees with the statement, then you should choose the 'explicitly contradicted' option. 'Implicitly contradicted' means that there is no direct evidence that disagrees with the statement but, reading between the lines, you believe that the statement is the opposite of the intended meaning of the text.

Example question (4 marks): read the statements below and, based on the evidence provided by the passage, decide whether:

- the statement is **supported** by the text **(S)**
- the statement is **implied** to be the case or is implicitly supported by the text **(I)**
- the text provides **no evidence** or information concerning the statement **(NE)**
- the statement is **implicitly contradicted** or implicitly refuted by the text **(IC)**
- the statement is **explicitly contradicted** or refuted by the text **(EC)**

a) Parents are being asked to make contributions to schools so that schools can buy simple necessities.

b) Some schools that may not be able to afford the essentials have money that is ring-fenced for school trips.

c) Pressure is put on parents so that the payment requests are seen as compulsory rather than optional.

d) Due to Ofsted pressure, schools are effectively writing off some children at a very early age.

5.9   Sequencing pieces of information

A question of this type may appear when the article presents events in a sequence, or the article mentions a process which has several steps. You will have a list of about seven options and you need to select three that are correct. In addition, rather than simply ticking them to confirm that they are correct, you need to state the order that these statements come in by dragging the words 'FIRST', 'SECOND' and 'THIRD' into the answer boxes in order to reflect the order in which the steps are taken.

Example question (3 marks): which of the following are three things a headteacher takes into consideration before an exclusion? Mark them as "FIRST", "SECOND" and "THIRD":

1. Consider whether appropriate support has been put in place for the pupil
2. Give the pupil a fidget spinner to assist with concentration
3. Pupils asked to give their side of the story
4. Invite the parents or carers in for a meeting
5. Establish if there are mitigating factors
6. Ensure that the pupil has served an appropriate number of detentions
7. Ensure that the pupil is aware of British values

Practice questions

In the mock tests in this book, you will see examples of all nine separate question types.

6.0 Exam Strategy

Here are a few final tips to help you succeed!

First of all, think about what time of day you work best and book a test time that suits you. So, if you are not a morning person, do not book a 9am test. Trying to read and understand a difficult reading comprehension text will not be easy if you aren't at your most alert! Give yourself plenty of time to arrive at the test centre, so that you are relaxed upon arrival. In the build-up to the test, it is preferable to be mentally preparing yourself for the task at hand, rather than to be worrying about whether or not you will arrive in time. If you are sitting the test at a centre that is not in your town, ensure that you have allowed additional time in case of public transport issues or in case the test centre is hard to find. Do bear in mind that the test centres are extremely busy in the month of August since most universities insist that the tests are passed before PGCE courses start in September, so book well in advance, or prepare for a long train ride to a test centre somewhere else in the country!

Prior to the test, you should not need to be doing any last-minute cramming. This is a time to relax and ensure you are as composed as possible. Read some articles from the education section of 'The Guardian' or articles from 'The Times Educational Supplement' to get yourself in the zone. You could even do some revision on the spellings of difficult words.

In the test itself, it is always the spelling that comes first. This part of the test is fairly straightforward and should not take up too much time. You should not be spending a whole minute per question: either you can spell the word or you can't! Don't waste time on the spelling section and look to get through it in about 5 minutes. Don't rush on this section though, but do be efficient. Do remember too that this is the only section in the test which you are not able to revisit.

The second part of the test is the punctuation section, and I would expect most people to pick up quite a few marks immediately and without too much thought. Finding all 15 punctuation omissions might require a bit more consideration, but if you follow my tips in the punctuation section of this book, then you have a systematic way to search for the missing pieces of punctuation. In an ideal word, this section can also be completed very efficiently and, even giving yourself plenty of time to check your work, you should have this section tied up in about 10 minutes. It is definitely worth checking this section, as you may later find that there is a sentence which might need a comma, or a word that might require a hyphen, which might take you from 15 to 16 changes, so you may need some time to think about which piece of punctuation you are then going to remove if you are going to go ahead and make this new change. Remember that this is the most important part of the test as there are always 15 marks available.

The third part of the test is the grammar section. In theory, this is the easiest part since the correct answers have already been given; it is just up to you to find them. In this section, sometimes the answer is obvious, especially if you are a native speaker, so don't worry if some of the questions seem almost too good to be true. Make sure you read the question and the answer options with care, so read slowly, making sure you read every word that is there, and making sure you haven't imagined words that are not there. For some of the more complicated questions, eliminate the obviously wrong answers and then compare the remaining answers. Which parts of the remaining answers are the same and which parts differ? Remember that in each task the questions are linked as they are all part of the same letter or document, so reading the previous question can provide better context for the question you might be struggling with. Again, this section should not take too long, perhaps 10 minutes, and can be returned to if you need to check over any questions you are not sure of.

It is quite possible that by this stage in the test, you have already done enough to secure a pass. However, don't walk out of the test centre just yet! Keep going and complete the reading comprehension (just to be on the safe side!). In my opinion, this is the hardest part of the test to prepare for and the hardest part of the test to take. Ideally, you will have only spent about 20 minutes so far on the other 3 sections, meaning you have over half the remaining time to dedicate to this section. Yes, you have completed 3 out of 4 sections, yes, you have only 10 – 12 more marks available, but in terms of effort, I would see the start of the reading comprehension as the half way point in the test. You will need to spend several minutes simply reading and re-reading the text. Do not worry about the clock ticking - concentrate on the text, try not to let your mind wander, and once you think you have a good understanding of what the text is about, start the questions. Read the questions as carefully as you read the text itself, and read all options when there are multiple-choice possibilities (the 'b' option may look like it's obviously the best answer, but read options 'c' and 'd' as well before committing). Some of the reading comprehension questions will be very challenging, and some of them may not have black and white answers either. However, if you have done your job on the spelling, punctuation and grammar, a few slightly ambiguous questions in the reading comprehension should not derail you too much and you should be leaving the test centre with your 'PASS' certificate!

I hope this book has been of use to you. Do take a look at the QTS Literacy Tutor website at www.qtsliteracytutor.co.uk where there is a free literacy test (different from the 3 mock tests in this book) and other resources to help you prepare for the final exam.

Good luck!

Mock test 1 (45 marks)

Spelling (10 marks)

1. As a _____, Gabrielle will be placed on tutor report from Monday. (consecuence / consiquence / consicuance / consequence)

2. Charlie was a very _____ boy, with plenty of friends. (likable / likeable / likabel / likeabel)

3. The chemistry teacher _____ dropped the bottle of sulphuric acid. (accidentally / acidentaly / accidentaly / accidentelly)

4. To be a successful teacher, you need to be very _____ . (adaptible / adapteble / adaptable / adaptabel)

5. It was _____ that he would never reach his target of a grade 5. (aparent / apparent / apparrant / apparrent)

6. Simon may be quite _____, but he is producing good class work. (mischievious / mischeivous / mischievous / mischeivious)

7. I think the head boy needs to be well-spoken and _____ . (curteous / courteus / courteous / courtious)

8. As a form tutor, it is expected that you provide a _____ for all your tutees. (referance / referrance / reference / referrence)

9. The safeguarding policy needs to be reviewed _____ . (immediatley / imediately / immediatily / immediately)

10. For a three mark question, you are expected to write more than a simple _____ . (sentance / sentanse / sentence / sentense)

Punctuation (15 marks)

What is the new behaviour policy

We have adapted a policy from Chalfont School in wakefield. Chalfont School is a school with a proven track record of outstanding outcomes for their students. The Chalfont students often achieve nearly a grade higher than expectations. The students at Chalfont School are very similar to York Academy students in terms of: prior attainment; comprehensive mix social demographic Free School Meals; and EAL. The new system is based around the use of a planner for rewards and sanctions. Teachers record good work and behaviour in the planner, and they also record poor behaviour in the planner before recording a comment of poor behaviour in class, each student will be reminded of our roles and given an opportunity to make the right choice. Eight recorded instances of poor behaviour in any one week (for incidents which take place inside or outside the classroom will lead a student to be placed in Internal Exclusion. This will give the quiet 90% respite from disruption, making the point that poor behaviour wont be tolerated and must improve.

At the beginning of each week all students start again with a clean slate of zero comments we firmly believe this will allow teachers to teach in a way that will maximise progress allowing students to concentrate on learning in the classroom. We have modified the system and its rules after student and staff input and believe this system will be for the benefit of all

Grammar (10 marks)

Task A

The aim of the MFL department is to:

a) create confident and competent life-long language learners; develop and nurture a curiosity for language learning; embed grammatical awareness which can be applied to English; and developing an appreciation of cultural differences in the world.

b) create confident and competent life-long language learners; develop and nurture a curiosity for language learning; embed grammatical awareness which can be applied to English; and develop an appreciation of cultural differences in the world.

c) create confident and competent life-long language learners; develop and nurture a curiosity for language learning; embed grammatical awareness which can be applied to English; and to develop an appreciation of cultural differences in the world.

d) create confident and competent life-long language learners; to develop and nurture a curiosity for language learning; to embed grammatical awareness which can be applied to English; and to develop an appreciation of cultural differences in the world.

We encourage students to apply their linguistic knowledge to understand and communicate confidently and effectively in a variety of situations. We work as a team

a) to deliver stimulating, challenging and enjoyable lessons that are accessible to all students and which enable them to realise their full potential.

b) for delivering stimulating, challenging and enjoyable lessons that are accessible to all students and which enable them to realise their full potential.

c) to deliver stimulating, challenging and enjoyable lessons that were accessible to all students and which enabled them to realise their full potential.

d) for delivering stimulating, challenging and enjoyable lessons that are accessible to all students and which are enabling them to realise their full potential.

At Kettlewick School, we strongly believe that learning a language can be good fun.

a) Furthermore, the ability to communicate in a foreign language is invaluable when applying for universities and jobs.

b) However, the ability to communicate in a foreign language is invaluable when applying for universities and jobs.

c) Besides, the ability to communicate in a foreign language is invaluable when applying for universities and jobs.

d) On the other hand, the ability to communicate in a foreign language is invaluable when applying for universities and jobs.

Task B

Glasgow Academy has an extremely successful Sixth Form, which has been in the top 10% for value-added for the last ten years. Our primary aim is

a) insuring that all students experience an academic education of the highest standard, and the school would offer a highly supportive environment for students to continue their post-sixteen studies.

b) to ensure that all students experience an academic education of the highest standard, and the school offers a highly supportive environment for students to continue their post-sixteen studies.

c) to insure that all students experience an academic education of the highest standard, and the school offers a highly supportive environment for students to continue their post-sixteen studies.

d) to ensure that all students experience an academic education of the most high standard, and the school offers a highly supportive environment for students to continue their post-sixteen studies.

Girls

a) should be welcome in our Sixth Form,
b) would be welcome in our Sixth Form,
c) might be welcome in our Sixth Form,
d) are welcome in our Sixth Form,

either as part of the consortium or as an external applicant.

In the Sixth Form,

a) we have high expectations, with senior students expected to operate as a role model for students in the lower school.

b) our expectations are high, with senior students expected to operate as role models for students in the lower school.

c) we have high expectations, and we expect senior students to operate as role models for students in the lower school.

d) our expectations are high, with senior students expecting to operate as role models for students in the lower school.

This is reflected in the Sixth Form appearance policy.

a) Boys are expected to dress in a smart business attire, with a suit, tie, and brown or black shoes compulsory. Girls are also expected to dress in a smart business style.

b) Boys are expected to dress in attire, with a smart business suit, tie, and brown or black shoes compulsory. Girls also are expected to dress in a smart business style.

c) Boys are expected to dress in a smart business attire, with a suit, tie, and brown or black shoes compulsory. Girls are also expected to dress in a business style which is smart.

d) Boys are expected to dress in a smart attire for business, with a suit, tie, and brown or black shoes compulsory. Girls are also expected to dress in a smart business style.

Task C

We have just told your child's school that we will inspect it on 13 November 2018. We are writing to you

a) although we would like to know what you think about the school.
b) although we would have liked to know what you think about the school.
c) because we would like to know what you think about the school.
d) because we would like to know what you might think about the school.

You can tell us your views about the school by completing Ofsted's online survey, Parent View.   Parent View asks for your opinion on 12 aspects of your child's school, including

a) the progress made by your child, how good you judge the teaching, and how the school deals with bullying and poor behaviour.
b) the progress your child has made, the quality of teaching, and how the school deals with bullying and poor behaviour.
c) the progress made by your child, the quality of teaching, and what the school does when there is bullying and poor behaviour.
d) the progress made by your child, the quality of teaching, and how the school deals with bullying and poor behaviour.

It also provides a free-text box for you to make additional comments, if you wish. The inspectors will use the online survey responses when inspecting your child's school.

a) Written comments can also be sent to the school in a sealed, confidential envelope, and addressed to the inspection team.

b) Written comments can also be sent to the school, marked confidential and addressed to the inspection team in a sealed envelope.

c) Written comments marked confidential can also be sent to the school in a sealed envelope, and addressed to the inspection team.

d) Written comments can also be sent to the school in a sealed envelope, marked confidential, and addressed to the inspection team.

Reading comprehension (10 marks)

School funding has always been an enormous talking point in the world of politics ever since wholesale reforms were made to the British education system back in 1944 when, due to the abysmal lack of education that many children had received, the government introduced free, and compulsory, education to all up to the age of 15.   However, it seems that in the current financial climate, perhaps using Brexit as an excuse, these 'free' schools are routinely asking for parental contributions in order to compensate for the chronic funding shortfall they are being forced to come to terms with. These parental contributions are not being used to top up teachers' salaries or to build new classrooms, but to spend on the "little extras", as the chancellor, Philip Hammond, in his recent budget described the luxuries our spoilt children enjoy these days – things like the most basic of school equipment: pens, pencils, and exercise books.

It seems that schools are becoming increasingly reliant on these parental offerings with a recent report stating that 43% of parents have been asked to make financial contributions, a figure up from 37% two years ago. Their proliferation is hard to ignore.

Whereas in the past, letters were polite in tone and were simply requesting a token, and obviously voluntary, payment of a couple of pounds per term, some schools are sending letters which resemble the sort of letters you would expect a debt collecting agency to scribe. Letters have been sent asking parents to set up a direct debit of £12.50 per month per pupil, or a one-off payment of £140 per year, making the latter seem like a tantalising bargain. Payment instructions have often been written in bold and underlined type, just to really emphasise the point. What's more, if parents have the audacity to ignore these requests to pay for the 'free' education on offer, failure to pay letters are swift to follow. Some schools have compared their voluntary payment schemes to those of other schools in order to demonstrate how generous their current offer is. What a bargain to only have to pay £450 per academic year for your three children's 'free' education when the school down the road is charging in excess of £500.

How does a school that is reliant on parental contributions, a school that struggles to pay for the basics such as textbooks and interactive whiteboards, meet the increasingly rigorous demands of Ofsted? How does a school in this position expect to keep hold of its most important asset, its teachers, if teachers are unable to deliver high-quality education because it cannot afford the appropriate classroom tools? It has been reported that in some schools, class sizes have increased and certain subjects are no longer offered as they are not profitable, with the result that the Arts, and even modern languages, are no longer on the academic menu because schools are pooling all their resources into the Holy Land of maths, English and science. Children with little hope of passing these subjects have been discarded, being placed into 'sink sets' where they simply fester so that a school can ensure that its higher performers meets the school's required performance data without being held back by the less able.

There has been a long battle about the existence of grammar schools and how they are pooling the best academic talent to the detriment of local comprehensive schools, but in the current climate, exactly the same thing is occurring within local comprehensive schools where intellectual segregation is a reality. A school that can't afford pencils is not going to offer a Duke of Edinburgh Award Scheme or a field trip to Swanage, never mind Iceland.

Some schools are taking things to the other extreme where the most academic pupils are being put on the conveyor belt towards GCSE and A level success and being scrubbed up for top universities. Such pupils are offered myriad opportunities which are simply not available to those not in the club. We have recently seen a school organise a trip to Borneo. Sounds great and, at £3,000 a place, it probably would be. Trips of this nature are only available to the select few, those who can afford to pay, therefore achieving class segregation through seemingly voluntary exclusion.

Nothing can match the trips organised by Eton, however, some of whose pupils went on a red carpet trip to meet President Putin. Not quite the same type of experience as a trip to Dartmoor to measure pieces of granite, but you get what you pay for I guess. The gap between state school pupils and those at the most elite private schools is the biggest inequality of all, with no other country in the world having a bigger equality gap than Britain.

Task 1 (2 marks): select two most appropriate titles for this article:

- Debt collectors employed in state schools
- Cost of school trips spiralling out of control
- Parents asked to cover funding shortfall
- School trips cancelled due to Brexit
- Free education disappearing before our eyes
- Equality in state sector schools at last
- Ofsted says parents to pay for compulsory text books
- Schools requesting parental contributions judged 'outstanding'

Task 2 (2 marks): the following groups might all be potential audiences or readers of the article, although some of them would find it more useful than others. Which group would find it the most relevant and which group would find it the least relevant?

- Primary school teachers
- Teachers that organise overseas trips
- Ofsted inspectors
- Parents of school children
- Pastoral staff
- Heads of year
- Headteachers
- Debt collecting agencies

Task 3 (2 marks): select the most appropriate alternative for each phrase as it appears in the context of the passage.

1. 'their proliferation is hard to ignore' (paragraph 2) is closest in meaning to:

   a) it is easy to see that they are becoming more popular
   b) we can't pretend to not see how important they are
   c) it is difficult to not notice how common they are
   d) ignoring is difficult due to their decrease

2. 'achieving class segregation through seemingly voluntary exclusion' (paragraph 6) is closest in meaning to:

   a) managing to keep students in a class apart by allowing them to rule themselves out
   b) managing to segregate a class by allowing pupils to decide whether or not they want to be in it or not
   c) managing to segregate a class by allowing students to decide whether they should be permanently excluded from school or not
   d) managing to keep students in a school apart if they refuse to volunteer

Task 4 (4 marks): read the statements below and, based on the evidence provided by the passage, decide whether:

- the statement is **supported** by the text **(S)**
- the statement is **implied** to be the case or is implicitly supported by the text **(I)**
- the text provides **no evidence** or information concerning the statement **(NE)**
- the statement is **implicitly contradicted** or implicitly refuted by the text **(IC)**
- the statement is **explicitly contradicted** or refuted by the text **(EC)**

a) Parents are being asked to make contributions to schools so that schools can buy simple necessities.

b) Some schools that may not be able to afford the essentials have money that is ring-fenced for school trips.

c) Pressure is put on parents so that the payment requests are seen as compulsory rather than optional.

d) Due to Ofsted pressure, schools are effectively writing off some children at a very early age.

Mock test 1 answers (45 marks, pass mark 30)

Spelling

1. As a **consequence**, Gabrielle will be placed on tutor report from Monday.
2. Charlie was a very **likeable** boy, with plenty of friends.
3. The chemistry teacher **accidentally** dropped the bottle of sulphuric acid.
4. To be a successful teacher, you need to be very **adaptable**.
5. It was **apparent** that he would never reach his target of a grade 5.
6. Simon may be quite **mischievous**, but he is producing good class work.
7. I think the head boy needs to be well-spoken and **courteous**.
8. As a form tutor, it is expected that you provide a **reference** for all your tutees.
9. The safeguarding policy needs to be reviewed **immediately**.
10. For a three mark question, you are expected to write more than a simple **sentence**.

Punctuation (15 marks)

What is the new behaviour policy? **(Add a question mark since this is a question.)**

We have adapted a policy from Chalfont School in Wakefield **(capital W for Wakefield because this is a place)**. Chalfont School is a school with a proven track record of outstanding outcomes for their students. The Chalfont students often achieve nearly a grade higher than expectations. The students at Chalfont School are very similar to York Academy students in terms of: prior attainment; comprehensive mix; **(add semicolon in this complicated list.**

It should be obvious that a semicolon is required and not a comma since the first item has a semicolon after it) social demographic (add semicolon in this complicated list) Free School Meals; and EAL.

(New paragraph as this section talks about how the new system is going to work, while paragraph one is an introduction explaining where the new behaviour policy came from.) The new system is based around the use of a planner for rewards and sanctions. Teachers record good work and behaviour in the planner, and they also record poor behaviour in the planner. (Add full stop as the next part is a new idea, so therefore a new sentence.) Before (capital B for the start of a new sentence) recording a comment of poor behaviour in class, each student will be reminded of our roles, (add a comma before coordinating preposition 'and') and given an opportunity to make the right choice. Eight recorded instances of poor behaviour in any one week (for incidents which take place inside or outside the classroom) (brackets have been opened but not closed around this extra bit of clarifying information) will lead a student to be placed in Internal Exclusion. This will give the quiet 90% respite from disruption, making the point that poor behaviour won't (contraction which requires an apostrophe) be tolerated and must improve.

At the beginning of each week, (add a comma after this introductory phrase where the reader can pause for breath) all students start again with a clean slate of zero comments. (Add a full stop as this is the end of one idea and the start of a new idea.) We (capital letter for the first word of a new sentence) firmly believe this will allow teachers to teach in a way that will maximise progress, (add a comma before this additional piece of information where the reader can pause for breath) allowing students to concentrate on

158

learning in the classroom. We have modified the system and its rules after student and staff input and believe this system will be for the benefit of all. **(Add a full stop at the end of this sentence / paragraph.)**

Grammar (10 marks)

Task A – b, a, a

Task B – b, d, b, a

Task C – c, d, d

Task A

The aim of the MFL department is to:

a) create confident and competent life-long language learners; develop and nurture a curiosity for language learning; embed grammatical awareness which can be applied to English, and developing an appreciation of cultural differences in the world. *(There is no consistency in the verb forms. All the verb forms need to make sense after the word 'to'.)*

b) **create confident and competent life-long language learners; develop and nurture a curiosity for language learning; embed grammatical awareness which can be applied to English, and develop an appreciation of cultural differences in the world.**

c) create confident and competent life-long language learners; develop and nurture a curiosity for language learning; embed grammatical awareness which can be applied to English, and to develop an appreciation of cultural differences in the world. *(Since there is the word 'to' in the question opener, the word 'to' is not required before 'develop'. None of the other verbs are preceded by 'to'.)*

d) create confident and competent life-long language learners; to develop and nurture a curiosity for language learning; to embed grammatical awareness which can be applied to English, and to develop an appreciation of cultural differences in the world. *(Since there is the word 'to' in the question opener, the word 'to' is not required before 'develop', 'embed' and the second 'develop'.)*

We encourage students to apply their linguistic knowledge to understand and communicate confidently and effectively in a variety of situations. We work as a team

a) **to deliver stimulating, challenging and enjoyable lessons that are accessible to all students and which enable them to realise their full potential.**

b) for delivering stimulating, challenging and enjoyable lessons that are accessible to all students and which enable them to realise their full potential. *(It is simply not correct English to say 'for delivering'.)*

c) to deliver stimulating, challenging and enjoyable lessons that were accessible to all students and which enabled them to realise their full potential. *(The present tense should be used because we are talking in general here and not referring to events in the past.)*

d) for delivering stimulating, challenging and enjoyable lessons that are accessible to all students and which are enabling them to realise their full potential. *(It is simply not correct English to say 'for delivering'. The present continuous 'are enabling' is not correct either as we are not talking about what is happening right now, we are talking in general, so the present tense is required.)*

At Kettlewick School, we strongly believe that learning a language can be good fun.

a) **Furthermore, the ability to communicate in a foreign language is invaluable when applying for universities and jobs.**

b) However, the ability to communicate in a foreign language is invaluable when applying for universities and jobs. *('However' does not make sense as this is not a contrasting statement.)*

c) Besides, the ability to communicate in a foreign language is invaluable when applying for universities and jobs. *(You could argue that 'besides' makes sense here, but the word 'furthermore' is better and is also more formal than 'besides', which sounds a bit too informal in this context.)*

d) On the other hand, the ability to communicate in a foreign language is invaluable when applying for universities and jobs. *('On the other hand' does not make sense as this is not a contrasting statement.)*

Task B

Glasgow Academy has an extremely successful Sixth Form, which has been in the top 10% for value-added for the last ten years. Our primary aim is

a) insuring that all students experience an academic education of the highest standard, and the school would offer a highly supportive environment for students to continue their post-sixteen studies. *('Insuring' is not the correct verb. It is the verb 'to ensure' that is needed in this example.)*

b) **to ensure that all students experience an academic education of the highest standard, and the school offers a highly supportive environment for students to continue their post-sixteen studies.**

c) to insure that all students experience an academic education of the highest standard, and the school offers a highly supportive environment for students to continue their post-sixteen studies. *('To insure' is not the correct verb. It is the verb 'to ensure' that is needed in this example.)*

d) to ensure that all students experience an academic education of the most high standard, and the school offers a highly supportive environment for students to continue their post-sixteen studies. *('The most high' is incorrect. This is a one syllable word and would therefore have a superlative form of 'the highest'.)*

Girls

a) should be welcome in our Sixth Form, *(Why 'should'? Is it not certain that they will be welcome?)*

b) would be welcome in our Sixth Form, *(Why 'would'? What needs to happen for them to be welcome?)*

c) might be welcome in our Sixth Form, *(Why 'might'? Is it not certain that they will be welcome?)*

d) **are welcome in our Sixth Form,**

either as part of the consortium or as an external applicant.

In the Sixth Form,

a) we have high expectations, with senior students expected to operate as a role model for students in the lower school. *(The sentence is more or less OK, but 'as a role model' doesn't really work with 'students' in the plural form. 'Our expectations are high' also sounds more formal because it is less personal than 'we have high expectations'.)*

b) **our expectations are high, with senior students expected to operate as role models for students in the lower school.**

c) we have high expectations, and we expect senior students to operate as role models for students in the lower school. *('Our expectations are high' sounds more formal because it is less personal than 'we have high expectations'. The 'and we' is a bit repetitive, so the language here is not very concise.)*

d) our expectations are high, with senior students expecting to operate as role models for students in the lower school. *(The verb form 'expecting' does not make grammatical sense in this sentence.)*

This is reflected in the Sixth Form appearance policy.

a) **Boys are expected to dress in smart business attire, with a suit, tie, and brown or black shoes compulsory. Girls are also expected to dress in a smart business style.**

b) Boys are expected to dress in attire, with a smart business suit, tie, and brown or black shoes compulsory. Girls also are expected to dress in a smart business style. *('To dress in attire' is completely meaningless.)*

c) Boys are expected to dress in a smart business attire, with a suit, tie, and brown or black shoes compulsory. Girls are also expected to dress in a business style which is smart. *('which is smart' does make sense, but this sentence is not concise enough and 'smart business style' would be better English.)*

d) Boys are expected to dress in a smart attire for business, with a suit, tie, and brown or black shoes compulsory. Girls are also expected to dress in a smart business style. *(You can dress in 'smart attire for business' but not in 'a smart attire for business'. Besides 'smart business attire' in option A is far more concise.)*

Task C

We have just told your child's school that we will inspect it on 13 November 2018. We are writing to you

a) although we would like to know what you think about the school.
   (*'Although' is the wrong word to link the two phrases.*)

b) although we would have liked to know what you think about the school.
   (*'Although' is the wrong word to link the two phrases. The visit has not yet happened so the past conditional tense of 'would have liked' makes no sense here.*)

c) **because we would like to know what you think about the school.**

d) because we would like to know what you might think about the school.
   (*You could argue that this makes sense, but the word 'might' sounds a bit out of place and it is hard to justify that this option sounds better than option C.*)

You can tell us your views about the school by completing Ofsted's online survey, Parent View. Parent View asks for your opinion on 12 aspects of your child's school, including

a) the progress made by your child, how good you judge the teaching, and how the school deals with bullying and poor behaviour. (*'How good you judge the teaching' is correct English but 'the quality of teaching' is more concise and more formal.*)

b) the progress your child has made, the quality of teaching, and how the school deals with bullying and poor behaviour. (*'The progress your child has made' is correct English but 'the progress made by your child' is more formal.*)

c) the progress made by your child, the quality of teaching, and what the school does when there is bullying and poor behaviour. *('What the school does when there is bullying' is correct English but 'how the school deals with bullying' is more concise and more formal.)*

d) **the progress made by your child, the quality of teaching, and how the school deals with bullying and poor behaviour.**

It also provides a free-text box for you to make additional comments, if you wish. The inspectors will use the online survey responses when inspecting your child's school.

a) Written comments can also be sent to the school in a sealed, confidential envelope, and addressed to the inspection team. *(It is not the envelope that is confidential, but the contents of the envelope.)*

b) Written comments can also be sent to the school, marked confidential and addressed to the inspection team in a sealed envelope. *(The phrase 'marked confidential' needs to be attached to 'envelope' since it is the envelope that is marked confidential.)*

c) Written comments marked confidential can also be sent to the school in a sealed envelope, and addressed to the inspection team. *(It is the envelope and not the written comments that need to be marked confidential.)*

d) **Written comments can also be sent to the school in a sealed envelope, marked confidential, and addressed to the inspection team.**

Reading comprehension (10 marks)

Task 1 answers

Parents asked to cover funding shortfall

Free education disappearing before our eyes

Task 2 answers

Headteachers – most relevant

Debt collecting agencies – least relevant

Task 3 answers

1 – c

2 - a

Task 4 answers

a) S   b) NE   c) S   d) I

Mock test 2 (47 marks)

Spelling (10 marks)

1. No teacher can _____ that every student will achieve their target grade. (guarantee / guarrantee / guarentee / guarantey)

2. The boy's progress in French was barely _____. (noticable / noticeable / noticeabel / notiseable)

3. The twins in year 6 do bear some _____. (ressemblance / resemblance / resemblence / ressemblence)

4. Teachers are very _____ to illness towards the end of the autumn term. (susceptible / suseptible / suseptable / susceptable)

5. My _____ is that you should complete the mock tests from our website. (reccommendation / recomendation / recommendation / recomendation)

6. Gareth is going to be _____ to the local Pupil Referral Unit. (transfered / transferred / transferd / tranzferd)

7. Vandalism used to be a rare _____ in this school. (ocurrence / occurence / ocurence / occurrence)

8. I am very _____ with your son's attitude in German at the moment. (disatisfied / dissatissfied / dissatisfyed / dissatisfied)

9. If teachers are _____ with certain classroom rules, they are more likely to win the respect of some of our challenging students. (flexable / flexiblel / flexabel / flexible)

10. The school minibus is out of action this week for _____. (mainternance / mainternence / maintenance / maintenence)

Punctuation (15 marks)

Able Interested and Motivated AIM) Policy

Principles of the policy:

All students should be encouraged and challenged to achieve their full potential through a differentiated broad and balanced curriculum this should occur within the classroom, and through identification and provision of additional pathways, including extra-curricular activities.

Definitions

The DfE promotes the figure of the top 10% of the schools population for the cohort of gifted and talented (G&T) students in the school. Gifted are the potential high performers in traditionally 'academic fields of study; talented are the potentially high performers in the arts music and sports. Able students will be identified by their potential to progress on to the G&T register within St boniface Roman Catholic School.

Name change:

The name change to AIM is not a branding gimmick: it reflects the new direction of the school as regards to its provision for gifted' students. The addition of interested and motivated gives a much greater fluidity to the process, and seeks to include students with an engaged passion for a subject even if they are not in the top 10% of the whole school cohort

aims:

The aims of this new policy are to provide a more challenging experience for students in all subject areas; to improve levels of attainment and motivation of the AIM to ensure staff are equipped to recognise and effectively cater for the AIM; to provide appropriate learning support and pastoral care; and to break down any barriers to learning and reduce underachievement.

Grammar (10 marks)

Task A

Dear Mr Parkinson,

Following my visit to the school on 7 February 2017, I write on behalf of Her Majesty's Chief Inspector of Education, Children's Services and Skills to report the inspection findings.

a) The visit was the first short inspection carried out since the school had been judged to be good in May 2013.

b) The visit was the first short inspection that was carried out since the school was judged to be good in May 2013.

c) The visit was the first short inspection carried out since the school was judged to be good in May 2013.

d) The visit was the first short inspection we carried out since the school was judged by us to be good in May 2013.

This school continues to be good. The leadership team has maintained the good quality of education in the school.

a) Since the previous inspection, you and the leadership team have worked effectively to further improve the standard of education provided for pupils.

b) Since the previous inspection, you and the leadership team worked effectively to further improve the standard of education provided for pupils.

c) Since the previous inspection, you and the leadership team should have worked effectively to further improve the standard of education provided for pupils.

d) Since the previous inspection, you and the leadership team must have worked effectively to further improve the standard of education provided for pupils.

Staff are proud of the work they do. Building on the long-standing traditions of the school, staff support the development of 'courteous, respectful and calm' young men, reflecting the school's well-established values.

In the sixth form,

a) students have access to a wide range of extra-curricular opportunities and are affective role models for younger pupils.

b) students have access to a wide range of extra-curricular opportunities and are effected role models for younger pupils.

c) students have access to a wide range of extra-curricular opportunities and are affected role models for younger pupils.

d) students have access to a wide range of extra-curricular opportunities and are effective role models for younger pupils.

Task B

We are delighted that you are considering applying to Devonport School's Sixth Form. As a Sixth Form we are committed to

a) ensuring that our Christian values, outstanding care for the individual and excellent student achievement, remains at the heart of our provision.
b) ensuring that our Christian values, outstanding care for the individual and excellent student achievement, remain at the heart of our provision.
c) ensure that our Christian values, outstanding care for the individual and excellent student achievement, remain at the heart of our provision.
d) ensure that our Christian values, outstanding care for the individual and excellent student achievement, remains at the heart of our provision.

This next step on your educational journey is an extremely important one.

There is no better feeling than seeing our

a) students achieve the grades and qualifications to move on to university, apprenticeships or the world of work.
b) students achieving the grades and qualifications to move on to university, apprenticeships or a world of work.
c) students achieve the grades and qualifications to move on to university, apprenticeships or the working world.
d) students who achieve the grades and qualifications to move on to university, apprenticeships or the world of work.

Our friendly Sixth Form community

a) is centred around strong relationships between staff and students who are built on mutual respect.

b) is centred around strong relationships between staff and students what are mutually built on respect.

c) is centred around strong relationships between staff and students which are built on mutual respect.

d) is centred around strong relationships between staff and students which are mutually built on respect.

It is

a) an environment where students, parents, guardians, and staff work in partnership to support your needs and allow you to fulfil your potential.

b) an environment in which students, parents, guardians, and staff work in partnership in order to support your needs and will allow you to fulfil your potential.

c) an environment where students, parents, guardians, and staff work in partnership to support your needs and allowing you to fulfil your potential.

d) an environment in which students, parents, guardians, and staff work in partnership to support your needs and allow you to fulfil your potential.

Task C

Mathematics at A level

a) is one of the most rewarding, satisfying and respected subjects available to a student.

b) is one of the most rewarding, most satisfying and most respected subjects available to a student.

c) is one of the most rewarding, satisfying, respected and available subjects to a student.

d) is one of the most rewarding, satisfying and respected subjects to an available student.

Alongside the general entry requirements to Sixth Form,

a) students should of achieved

b) students should have achieved

c) students could have achieved

d) students could of achieved

at least a Grade 6 in GCSE Maths and have at least a grade 5 in two Science GCSEs.

During the Mathematics A Level, students will study three specific areas: pure mathematics, statistics and mechanics. These will be examined in three papers,

a) the first two of which will focus on the pure content and the third will cover both statistics and mechanics.

b) the first two of which focus on the pure content and the third will cover both statistics and mechanics.

c) the first two of which focuses on the pure content and the third will cover both statistics and mechanics.

d) the first two of which will focus on the pure content and the third covers both statistics and mechanics.

Reading comprehension (12 marks)

I recently overheard a revealing conversation take place among a group of Year 9 boys. Waiting for a modern languages lesson to begin, the lads were discussing the relevance of studying French at school today. Sadly, their attitudes were uniformly negative. Doubting its long-term value to his life, one boy was convinced that within months of finishing the course, he would have forgotten all the French vocabulary he had been taught. His friends responded with similar comments. Since there is no way of knowing whether these particular teenagers are representative of Britain's pupil population as a whole, it is unwise to assume that the views of the observed individuals are typical, or even widespread, but we can still conclude that, as far as some youngsters are concerned, the extent to which they feel it is important to study a subject purposefully is proportional to that subject's perceived utility.

Few areas taught in schools are as relevant to the lives of young people as information literacy (IL) - that body of knowledge, skills and understanding required by a person to find sound information effectively and use it appropriately to resolve the situation that prompted its acquisition. Even the most apathetic of young people must surely concede that we all need and indeed pursue information. In addition, we frequently hear teenagers express lively views about the value of certain kinds of resources and individual materials, like, for example, particular websites, and how information can best be found. It is often said that, since virtually every other adult in Britain has attended school, the majority feel sufficiently well informed to be able to give an opinion on education; we may reach a similar conclusion with regards to people's perspectives on information.

The challenge for an educator intent on promoting IL (Information Literacy) does not, then, lie in establishing the importance of information in the learner's life. Rather, since information is now so easy to access and transfer from a source document to one's own work, the key issue is that of justifying to pupils and, on occasions, the senior leadership team within a school, why whole lessons should be devoted to IL. The case is not helped by the fact that, in the current educational climate, youngsters with limited information skills can still gain a reasonable degree of academic success at school. Even if it were possible to make a firm connection between scholarly achievement and the need for IL, however, by secondary age some pupils are so turned off by education and all it involves that these messages would be unlikely to motivate everyone. There are, of course, other cards that can be played. These can be summarised as follows:

In introducing IL to students emphasise:

- that it is essential if we are to comprehend properly local and global issues
- its importance if we are to make appropriate and informed decisions as a consumer and citizen
- that it helps us in our efforts to retrain in order to ensure continued employability in a changing workplace
- that it gives us the tools we need for lifelong learning
- that it provides the means for us to find out more about matters of personal interest

The final option may provide the most fruitful avenue for the teacher. If learners can understand the various principles of IL in terms that are relevant to their own interests and come to realise effective information behaviour

can aid them in their quest to find out more about matters that are important to them personally, the teachers arguments in favour of good practice are more likely to be accepted. We should not dismiss, either, the educational value of allowing youngsters to conduct detailed study of an area that interests them. According to Junko and Cotton, even when information-seeking is not prompted by school work, "the behaviour of and motivations for searching the information online relate to academic pursuits". Indeed, having the curiosity to search for information is becoming a beginning stage in the academic research process. Carmichael takes a similar stance, arguing that "serious study" can include the investigation of a matter of personal interest.

Given the information is pivotal to independent learning and this is a process which is, of course, central to education itself, it is surprising that the discipline of IL is not more widely recognised in schools. In fact even the phrase "information literacy" itself may be unfamiliar to some readers. Crucially, however, IL teaching can help tackle problems that are all too common. Anyone who has watched pupils pursue a heavily formulaic approach to finding and using information will be aware that such a simplistic method is far from ideal. IL can help remedy this inadequacy, lead to the eradication of other process deficiencies and contribute to improved outcomes; for example, the information literate learner will submit work that is genuinely his or her own (rather than plagiarise) and it will be the product of an understanding that has been gained from a pool of high quality resources (not a few chosen simply because they would seem at first glance to be relevant). And of course, since so much dubious material is available via the web, for some commentators the greatest attraction of IL is that it promotes a more critical mindset.

Task A (2 marks): select the most appropriate alternative for each phrase as it appears in the context of the passage:

1. "to study a subject purposefully is proportional to that subject's perceived utility" is closest in meaning to:

    a) to study a subject with interest depends on how useful the person feels the subject is

    b) to study a subject that is useful depends on how interesting you find it

    c) to study a subject to the best of your ability depends on its purpose

    d) to study a subject well depends on the proportion of your time that you spend on it

2. "Even the most apathetic of young people must surely concede" is closest in meaning to:

a) even the weakest of young people has to believe

b) even the most indifferent of young people has to admit

c) even the most feeble of young people must confess

d) even the most enthusiastic of young people has to surrender

Task B (4 marks): select the four most appropriate statements to complete the bulleted list which appears in the passage. An example has already been done for you:

In introducing IL to students emphasise:

-

-

- that it helps us in our efforts to retrain in order to ensure continued employability in a changing workplace

-

-

a) that it is imperative for us to gain a sound understanding of what is going on in the world

b) that it can help us in our quest to become more educated

c) that there is more to computers than social media

d) that it is imperative to be fluent with everyday packages that are used in business

e) how crucial it is in order for us to make good choices in everyday situations and when making purchases

f) how important it is to improve our general literacy

g) that is enables us to learn more about the things which appeal to us

h) that it enables us to stay on top of current affairs

Task C (4 marks): select the four statements that are true:

a) Everybody understands the term 'information literacy'

b) With poor information literacy skills, students may not be able to recognise whether the information they are reading can be trusted or not

c) Information literacy is probably one of the most relevant subjects taught in schools

d) Information literacy helps to assist boys appreciate the relevance of French

e) A good way to promote information literacy is to allow students to use it in an area that interests them

f) Promoting information literacy might result in fewer students submitting plagiarised work

g) Independent learning is rarely underpinned by information

h) The first thing educators need to do is convince people of the need for information before convincing them of the need for information literacy

Task D (2 marks): the following groups might all be potential audiences or readers of the article, although some of them would find it more useful than others. Which group would find it the most relevant and which group would find it the least relevant?

- Teachers of ICT
- Teachers of PSHE
- Headteachers
- Heads of department
- Form tutors
- Ofsted inspectors
- IT technicians

Mock test 2 answers (47 marks, pass mark 31)

Spelling (10 marks)

1. No teacher can **guarantee** that every student will achieve their target grade.

2. The boy's progress in French was barely **noticeable**.

3. The twins in year 6 do bear some **resemblance**.

4. Teachers are very **susceptible** to illness towards the end of the autumn term.

5. Gareth is going to be **transferred** to the local Pupil Referral Unit.

6. My **recommendation** is that you should complete the mock tests from our website.

7. Vandalism used to be a rare **occurrence** in this school.

8. I am very **dissatisfied** with your son's attitude in German at the moment.

9. If teachers are **flexible** with certain classroom rules, they are more likely to win the respect of some of our challenging students.

10. The school minibus is out of action this week for **maintenance**.

Punctuation (15 marks)

Able Interested and Motivated (AIM) **(an acronym for the policy has been added here inside brackets, but only the closing brackets have been added, so an opening set of brackets needs to be included)** Policy

Principles of the policy:

All students should be encouraged and challenged to achieve their full potential through a differentiated, broad **(a comma needs to be added between the two adjectives)** and balanced curriculum. **(A full stop needs to be added because one idea has ended and a new idea has been introduced. Idea one concerns students achieving their full potential, and idea two talks about where this is going to occur.)** This **('this' is now the first word of a new sentence, so should be capitalised)** should occur within the classroom, and through identification and provision of additional pathways, including extra-curricular activities.

Definitions: **(a colon needs to be added here to mirror all the other colons present in the other sub-headings)**

The DfE promotes the figure of the top 10% of the school's **(an apostrophe needs to be added here since it is the population belonging to the school)** population for the cohort of gifted and talented (G&T) students in the school. Gifted are the potential high performers in traditionally 'academic' **(the author has put an inverted comma before the word 'academic', but there is no inverted comma after this word or later in the sentence. The author has placed the inverted commas around this word to draw attention to it, so that is has a meaning of 'so-called'.)** fields of study; talented are the potentially high performers in the arts, **(a comma is required here to separate items in**

182

this short list) music and sports. Able students will be identified by their potential to progress on to the G&T register within St Boniface **(a capital letter is required for the name of the school)** Roman Catholic School.

Name change:

The name change to AIM is not a branding gimmick: it reflects the new direction of the school as regards its provision for 'gifted' **(this is a similar to the inverted comma used in the word 'academic' above. The author wishes to draw attention to the word 'gifted', giving it the meaning of 'so-called gifted students')** students. The addition of interested and motivated gives a much greater fluidity to the process, and seeks to include students with an engaged passion for a subject, **(a comma needs to be added here before this additional dependent clause is added. If you were reading the text, this is a place where you might naturally pause for breath, so you could justify a comma on this basis)** even if they are not in the top 10% of the whole school cohort. **(A full stop needs to be added here at the end of this sentence / paragraph.)**

Aims: **(A capital letter needs to be added since this is a title / sub-heading)**

The aims of this new policy are: **(a colon needs to be added here because a list follows. The colon needs to go before the word 'to' since all the other items in the list start with the word 'to')** to provide a more challenging experience for students in all subject areas; to improve levels of attainment and motivation of the AIM; **(a semicolon needs to be added here to separate items in this complicated list)** to ensure staff are equipped to recognise and effectively cater for the AIM; to provide appropriate learning support and pastoral care; and to break down any barriers to learning and reduce underachievement.

Grammar (10 marks)

Task A – c, a, d

Task B – b, a, c, d

Task C – a, b, a

Task A

Dear Mr Parkinson,

Following my visit to the school on 7 February 2017, I write on behalf of Her Majesty's Chief Inspector of Education, Children's Services and Skills to report the inspection findings.

a) The visit was the first short inspection carried out since the school had been judged to be good in May 2013. *(You could argue that the use of 'had been' is not incorrect, but 'was' in option 'c' is preferable and much more concise.)*

b) The visit was the first short inspection that was carried out since the school was judged to be good in May 2013. *(The sentence makes sense, but there is no need for the 'that was'.)*

c) **The visit was the first short inspection carried out since the school was judged to be good in May 2013.**

d) The visit was the first short inspection we carried out since the school was judged by us to be good in May 2013. *(This sentence also makes sense, but since this is an Ofsted report, they are much more likely to write in an impersonal style, so it is unlikely that they would refer to themselves as 'we'.)*

This school continues to be good. The leadership team has maintained the good quality of education in the school.

a) **Since the previous inspection, you and the leadership team have worked effectively to further improve the standard of education provided for pupils.**

b) Since the previous inspection, you and the leadership team worked effectively to further improve the standard of education provided for pupils. *('Worked' is incorrect in this example because you would use the simple past tense for an action that took place at a precise moment in the past.)*

c) Since the previous inspection, you and the leadership team should have worked effectively to further improve the standard of education provided for pupils. *(The sentence makes sense grammatically, but the statement says that the school 'continues to be good', so they are unlikely to mention things that the school has neglected to do in the very next sentence.)*

d) Since the previous inspection, you and the leadership team must have worked effectively to further improve the standard of education provided for pupils. *(The use of 'must have' doesn't sound like the sort of phrase that Ofsted would write in a report, even if it is grammatically correct.)*

Staff are proud of the work they do. Building on the long-standing traditions of the school, staff support the development of 'courteous, respectful and calm' young men, reflecting the school's well-established values.

In the sixth form,

a) students have access to a wide range of extra-curricular opportunities and are affective role models for younger pupils. *(Wrong spelling of the word 'effective'.)*

b) students have access to a wide range of extra-curricular opportunities and are effected role models for younger pupils. *('Effected' is the past tense of the verb 'to effect'. This word is meaningless in this context.)*

c) students have access to a wide range of extra-curricular opportunities and are affected role models for younger pupils. *('Affected' means 'influenced'. This word is meaningless in this context.)*

d) students have access to a wide range of extra-curricular opportunities and are effective role models for younger pupils.

Test B

We are delighted that you are considering applying to Devonport School's Sixth Form. As a Sixth Form we are committed to

a) ensuring that our Christian values, outstanding care for the individual and excellent student achievement, remains at the heart of our provision. *(There are three items as the subject, so the verb needs to be in the plural form to reflect this. 'Remains' is the verb in the singular form.)*

b) ensuring that our Christian values, outstanding care for the individual and excellent student achievement, remain at the heart of our provision.

c) ensure that our Christian values, outstanding care for the individual and excellent student achievement, remain at the heart of our provision. *('Ensure' does not make sense after the phrase 'we are committed to'.)*

d) ensure that our Christian values, outstanding care for the individual and excellent student achievement, remains at the heart of our provision. *('Ensure' does not make sense after the phrase 'we are committed to'. There are also three items as the subject, so the verb needs to be in the plural form to reflect this. 'Remains' is the verb in the singular form.)*

This next step on your educational journey is an extremely important one.

There is no better feeling than seeing our

a) **students achieve the grades and qualifications to move on to university, apprenticeships or the world of work.**

b) students achieving the grades and qualifications to move on to university, apprenticeships or a world of work. *('Than seeing our students achieving' is arguably correct, but 'achieve' is better. 'A world of work' does not make sense as there is only one world of work, so it should be referred to as 'the world of work'.)*

c) students achieve the grades and qualifications to move on to university, apprenticeships or the working world. *(The phrase 'the world of work' sounds more natural than 'the working world' which also has a slightly different meaning.)*

d) students who achieve the grades and qualifications to move on to university, apprenticeships or the world of work. *(The insertion of the word 'who' makes this a sentence that doesn't make sense. If you want to make 'who' work, then you would have to get rid of the word 'to', or put the 'who' clause inside commas and add an extra phrase at the end.)*

Our friendly Sixth Form community

a) is centred around strong relationships between staff and students who are built on mutual respect. *(It is the relationships that are built on mutual respect and not the students.)*

b) is centred around strong relationships between staff and students what are mutually built on respect. *('What' should never be used as a relative pronoun. It should also be 'who', 'that' or ' which'.)*

c) **is centred around strong relationships between staff and students which are built on mutual respect.**

d) is centred around strong relationships between staff and students which are mutually built on respect. *(It is the respect that is mutual and not the act of building.)*

It is

a) an environment where students, parents, guardians, and staff work in partnership to support your needs and allow you to fulfil your potential. *(This sentence is OK, but 'in which' in option 'd' is a bit more formal than 'where'.)*

b) an environment in which students, parents, guardians, and staff work in partnership in order to support your needs and will allow you to fulfil your potential. *(The words 'in order' are fine, but they can be removed to make this a more concise sentence.)*

c) an environment where students, parents, guardians, and staff work in partnership to support your needs and allowing you to fulfil your potential. *(The word 'allowing' is not grammatically correct. The verb form needs to mirror the verb form 'work'.)*

d) **an environment in which students, parents, guardians, and staff work in partnership to support your needs and allow you to fulfil your potential.**

Task C

Mathematics at A level

a)   **is one of the most rewarding, satisfying and respected subjects available to a student.**

b)   is one of the most rewarding, most satisfying and most respected subjects available to a student. *(The repetition of the word 'most' is ugly and unnecessary.)*

c)   is one of the most rewarding, satisfying, respected and available subjects to a student. *(The positioning of the adjective 'available' before 'subjects' affects the meaning of the sentence and it no longer makes sense.)*

d)   is one of the most rewarding, satisfying and respected subjects to an available student. *(It is the subjects that are available and not the students.)*

Alongside the general entry requirements to Sixth Form,

a)   students should of achieved *('Should of' is ugly and wrong.)*

b)   **students should have achieved**

c)   students could have achieved *(The phrase is grammatically correct, but the meaning is altered. If the students 'could have achieved', what was their reason for not achieving the level 6? It simply doesn't make sense.)*

d)   students could of achieved *('Could of' is ugly and wrong.)*

at least a Grade 6 in GCSE Maths and have at least a grade 5 in two Science GCSEs.

During the Mathematics A Level students will study three specific areas: pure mathematics, statistics and mechanics. These will be examined in three papers,

a) **the first two of which will focus on the pure content and the third will cover both statistics and mechanics.**

b) the first two of which focus on the pure content and the third will cover both statistics and mechanics. *(In the sentence, the future tense is being used. There is a lack of verb tense consistency here as 'focus' is in the present tense.)*

c) the first two of which focuses on the pure content and the third will cover both statistics and mechanics. *(In the sentence, the future tense is being used. There is a lack of verb tense consistency here as 'focus' is in the present tense. In addition, the singular verb form 'focuses' does not match the plural subject.)*

d) the first two of which will focus on the pure content and the third covers both statistics and mechanics. *(In the sentence, the future tense is being used. There is a lack of verb tense consistency here as 'covers' is in the present tense.)*

Reading comprehension (12 marks)

Task A

a, b

Task B

a, e, b, g

Task C

b, c, e, f

Task D

Most relevant – ICT teachers

Least relevant – IT technicians

Mock test 3 (45 marks)

Spelling (10 marks)

1. The girls excelled under Mr Tomkins as he was very _____ . (knowlidgeable / knowledgeable / knowledgable / knowledgeabel)

2. The algebra question in paper 3 was very _____ . (ambigous / ambiguos / ambiguous / ambiguouse)

3. You are not allowed to use a _____ in tomorrow's exam. (callculator / calcullater / calculater / calculator)

4. The policy in the school is that pupils should not wear any jewellery, with the exception of the Kara, which can be worn for _____ purposes. (riligious / relegious / religous / religious)

5. Asking a year 7 student to remain after school for a 1 hour detention is never _____ . (justifaible / justifible / justifyable / justifiable)

6. The exam last year was the toughest exam _____ . (imaginabel / imaginable / imaginible / imagineble)

7. The year 11s should be going into tomorrow's exam with a lot of _____ . (confidince / confidance / confidence / confadence)

8. A _____ of this type of behaviour will mean that Peter will have to work in isolation next week. (recurence / recurrence / recurrance / recurance)

9. The pupils who attained the highest grades were simply the most _____ throughout the course of the year. (committed / commited / comitted / comited)

10. There was a clear problem with _____ in the local primary school. (disipline / disiplin / discipline / disciplin)

Punctuation (15 marks)

Welcome to Fulham Academys Sixth Form

It is our aim to help you decide what you wish to do after completing your courses here we will then work to make sure that you achieve the necessary grades qualifications and experience needed to succeed in completing those objectives. The Sixth Form should be more than just a finishing school for university and work in our Sixth Form, you will have the chance to learn more study skills; develop personal qualities improve your time management; further extra-curricular interests; develop new sporting interests.

As a Sixth Former you are an integral part of the school. We expect you to take an active role in the school which will make this one of the most enjoyable periods of your life. Your time in the Sixth Form will pass very quickly and its important that you adjust to the demands of 16-19 education very quickly. You must remember that a key element of Sixth Form life is openness and honesty; if you are experiencing pastoral or academic difficulties causing you to be behind with deadlines, do not suffer in silence – come and talk to us. The school motto – "Together We Learn, Achieve and Succeed – is a good phrase to learn and remember while studying here.

Grammar (10 marks)

Task A

Dear Parent/Carer,

There is an exciting opportunity for your child to attend a residential trip to the beautiful and historic birthplace of Shakespeare, Stratford-Upon-Avon, from 7-9 December 2018. This trip will be run jointly between the English and Drama departments,

a) and will vastly enrich your childs' knowledge and skills in both subjects, whilst being great fun and providing them with lifelong memories.

b) and will vastly enrich your child's knowledge and skills in both subjects, whilst being great fun and providing them with lifelong memories.

c) vastly enriching your childs' knowledge and skills in both subjects, whilst being great fun and providing them with lifelong memories.

d) and will enrich your child's knowledge and skills vastly in both subjects, whilst being great fun and providing them with lifelong memories.

As your child will study a Shakespeare text as well as the Victorian classic novella, 'A Christmas Carol', for their English GCSE, we will be focusing on these areas to give your child the best head start we can,

a) whilst also provide them with unique opportunities far beyond the curriculum.

b) whilst also providing them with unique opportunities far beyond the curriculum.

c) whilst also providing them with opportunities far beyond the unique curriculum.

d) whilst also providing unique opportunities for them far beyond the curriculum.

This trip will be packed full with exciting activities and

a) will minimise any disruption to the rest of your child's subjects as they will miss only one day of school.
b) minimises any disruption to the rest of your child's subjects as they will miss only one day of school.
c) should minimise any disruption to the rest of your child's subjects as they will miss only one day of school.
d) minimises any disruption to the rest of your child's subjects as they are missing only one day of school.

Task B

At Wigan Academy, we strongly believe in the education of the whole child and having a broad and balanced curriculum that supports all learners.

a) Pupils wishing to gain an understanding of the modern world can do so through Travel & Tourism.
b) Pupils who wish to gain an understanding of the modern world can do so through Travel & Tourism.
c) Pupils that wish to gain an understanding of the modern world can do so through Travel & Tourism.
d) Pupils wish to gain an understanding of the modern world can do so through Travel & Tourism.

Our values-driven curriculum is enhanced further with an RE and PSHE curriculum that embraces the development of the whole child,

a) raises their awareness of all aspects of Spirituality, Social Justice, and Moral Conduct and supporting pupils to become well-rounded citizens ready to tackle the challenges of the modern world.

b) raises their awareness of all aspects of Spirituality, Social Justice, and Moral Conduct and supports pupils to become well-rounded citizens ready to tackle the challenges of the modern world.

c) raise their awareness of all aspects of Spirituality, Social Justice, and Moral Conduct and supporting pupils to become well-rounded citizens ready to tackle the challenges of the modern world.

d) raising their awareness of all aspects of Spirituality, Social Justice, and Moral Conduct, and supports pupils to become well-rounded citizens ready to tackle the challenges of the modern world.

Beyond the classroom, pupils have many opportunities

a) to deepen their love of learning, supported when they need support, and to gain stretch and challenge when they wish to go above and beyond the standard curriculum.

b) to deepen their love of learning, to be supported when they need support, and to gain stretch and challenge when they wish to go above and beyond the standard curriculum.

c) to deepen their love of learning, to be supported when they need support, and gaining stretch and challenge when they wish to go above and beyond the standard curriculum.

d) for deepening their love of learning, for being supported when they need support, and for gaining stretch and challenge when they wish to go above and beyond the standard curriculum.

Each child can expect to

a) be taught by a subject expert, who is continually challenging all learners to achieve there very best.

b) be taught by a subject expert, who will be continually challenging all learners to achieve their very best.

c) be taught by experts in the subject, who will be continually challenging all learners to achieve there very best.

d) be taught by a subject expert, who will be continually challenging all learners to their best achievement.

Task C

We are proud of our outstanding summer 2018 results, which build on the excellent results achieved in 2017 which placed the school in the top 5% nationally for student progress.

a) The outcome for both student progress and achievement evidence our distinctiveness and effectiveness as a Church of England School.

b) The outcomes for both student progress and achievement evidences our distinctiveness and effectiveness as a Church of England School.

c) The outcomes for both student progress and achievement evidence our distinctiveness and effectiveness as a Church of England School.

d) The outcomes for student progress and achievement both evidence our distinctiveness and effectiveness as a Church of England School.

The Attainment 8 score

a) gives an indication of the raw grades that students would have achieved in the qualifications that they studied.

b) gives an indication of the raw grades that students had achieved in the qualifications that they studied.

c) gives an indication of the raw grades that students will have achieved in the qualifications that they studied.

d) gives an indication of the raw grades that students have achieved in the qualifications that they studied.

However, this value is very much dependant on the academic ability of the cohort of students which is indicated by the APS on entry.

a) An academic cohort of students would achieve high grades yielding a large attainment 8 score but have a poor progress score.

b) An academic cohort of students could achieve high grades yielding a large attainment 8 score but have a poor progress score.

c) An academic cohort of students should achieve high grades yielding a large attainment 8 score but have a poor progress score.

d) An academic cohort of students achieves high grades yielding a large attainment 8 score but have a poor progress score.

Reading comprehension (10 marks)

There are two different types of exclusion, permanent and fixed term. A permanent exclusion means that the child is removed from the school roll. However, if the parents / carers appeal the exclusion and the matter is referred to an Independent Review Panel, the headteacher is not able to remove the pupil's name from the Admissions Register until the panel has reached an outcome. A fixed term exclusion if for a specified period of time. A pupil can be excluded multiple times in a single academic year, up to a maximum of 45 days in total.

There are certain circumstances in which a child can be excluded. A pupil can only be excluded on disciplinary grounds and the decision to exclude must be lawful, reasonable, fair and proportionate. In certain cases, the conduct of pupils outside of school may be considered as grounds for exclusion, however, this would normally be set out in the school's behaviour policy. This could be as a result of a child causing physical harm to another student outside of the school grounds, or bringing the name of the school into disrepute on the journey to / from school. Whether or not the pupil is wearing school uniform does not influence a decision to exclude a pupil.

A decision to permanently exclude a pupil should only be taken:

"in response to a serious breach or persistent breaches of the school's behaviour policy; and where allowing the pupil to remain in school would seriously harm the education or welfare of the pupil or others in the school".

Under the Equality Act 2010, schools must not discriminate against pupils because of their sex, race, disability, religion or belief, or sexual orientation, pregnancy or gender reassignment. For disabled children, this includes a duty to make 'reasonable adjustments' to policies and practices.

It is unlawful to exclude for a non-disciplinary reason. For example, it would be unlawful to exclude a pupil simply because they have additional needs or a disability that the school feels it is unable to meet. It would also be unlawful to exclude for a reason such as academic attainment / ability, the action of a pupil's parents, or the failure of a pupil to meet specific conditions before they are reinstated, such as attend a reintegration meeting.

However a headteacher could lawfully exclude a child for: repeated failure to follow academic instruction; failure to complete a behavioural sanction, e.g. a detention; repeated and persistent breaches of the school's behavioural policy. Even if the offence that has immediately led to the exclusion would not have normally constituted a serious enough breach on its own, a child can still be excluded if it is part of a wider pattern of behaviour.

The decision on whether to exclude is for a headteacher to take. Pupils should be given an opportunity to present their case before a decision is made.

When considering whether to exclude, headteachers should take account of any contributing factors identified after an incident of poor behaviour has occurred – for example, where it comes to light that a pupil has suffered bereavement, has mental health issues or has been subject to bullying.

The Statutory Guidance is clear that early intervention should be used to address underlying causes of disruptive behaviour. This should include:

- an assessment of whether appropriate support is in place to support any special educational needs or disability that a pupil may have;

- the use of a multi-agency assessment for pupils who demonstrate persistent disruptive behaviour.

The governing body has a duty to consider parents' representations about an exclusion. The extent of this duty and how it is exercised depend on the length and nature of the exclusion.

The following parties must be invited to a meeting of the governing body and allowed to make representations:

- parents;

- the headteacher; and

- a representative of the Local Authority (in the case of a maintained school or pupil referral unit)

In the light of their consideration, the Governing Body can either:

- uphold an exclusion; or

- direct reinstatement of the pupil immediately or on a particular date.

If the governing body uphold a permanent exclusion, parents have the right to request that their decision is reviewed by an Independent Review Panel (IRP).

Parents may request an Independent Review Panel even if they did not make a case to, or attend, the meeting at which the governing body considered the exclusion.

The panel can decide to:

- uphold the exclusion decision;

- recommend that the governing body reconsiders their decision; or

- quash the decision and direct that the governing body considers the exclusion again.

When considering the governing body's decision, the Panel should apply the following tests which need to be satisfied to quash the decision:

1. Did the headteacher and / or governing body act outside the scope of their legal powers in taking the decision to exclude?

2. Did the governing board rely on irrelevant points, fail to take account of all relevant points or make a decision so unreasonable that no governing board acting reasonably in such circumstances could have made it?

3. Was the process of exclusion and the governing body's consideration so unfair or flawed that justice was clearly not done?

If any of these criteria are met, the Panel can quash the decision of the governing body and direct that they consider the exclusion again.

Task A (3 marks): which of the following are three things a headteacher must take into consideration before an exclusion? Mark them as "FIRST", "SECOND" and "THIRD":

1.   Consider whether appropriate support has been put in place for the pupil
2.   Give the pupil a fidget spinner to assist with concentration
3.   Pupils asked to give their side of the story
4.   Invite the parents or carers in for a meeting
5.   Establish if there are mitigating factors
6.   Ensure that the pupil has served an appropriate number of detentions
7.   Ensure that the pupil is aware of British values

Task B (4 marks): which of the following are examples of legal exclusions (select 4 in total):

1.   a pupil has brought the school into disrepute at a local shopping centre
2.   a pupil has fallen pregnant despite being under the legal age
3.   a pupil has disabilities and the school is unable to provide support for the disability
4.   a pupil consistently displays a lack of compliance towards the school rules
5.   a pupil can be excluded for a minor offence
6.   a pupil poses a threat to others in the school community
7.   a pupil says he belongs to a gang outside of school
8.   a pupil consistently underachieves and fails all his end of year tests
9.   a pupil has committed a slightly less serious indiscretion, but has previously failed to meet the school's expectations on a repeated basis

Task C (3 marks): read the following questions and select which refer to:

- illegality
- irrationality
- procedural impropriety

1. Did the headteacher and / or governing body act outside the scope of their legal powers in taking the decision to exclude?
2. Did the governing board rely on irrelevant points, fail to take account of all relevant points or make a decision so unreasonable that no governing board acting reasonably in such circumstances could have made?
3. Was the process of exclusion and the governing body's consideration so unfair or flawed that justice was clearly not done?

Mock test 3 answers (45 marks, pass mark 30)

Spelling (10 marks)

1. The girls excelled under Mr Tomkins as he was very **knowledgeable**.

2. The algebra question in paper 3 was very **ambiguous**.

3. You are not allowed to use a **calculator** in tomorrow's exam.

4. The policy in the school is that pupils should not wear any jewellery, with the exception of the Kara, which can be worn for **religious** purposes.

5. Asking a year 7 student to remain after school for a 1 hour detention is never **justifiable**.

6. The exam last year was the toughest exam **imaginable**.

7. The year 11s should be going into tomorrow's exam with a lot of **confidence**.

8. A **recurrence** of this type of behaviour will mean that Peter will have to work in isolation next week.

9. The pupils who attained the highest grades were simply the most **committed** throughout the course of the year.

10. There was a clear problem with **discipline** in the local primary school.

Punctuation (15 marks)

Welcome to Fulham Academy's **(add an apostrophe as it is the Sixth Form that belongs to the Academy)** Sixth Form, **(add a comma here as this is a letter)**

It is our aim to help you decide what you wish to do after completing your courses here. **(Full stop as this is the end of an idea before the start of a new one.)** We **(capital letter for the first word in a new sentence)** will then work to make sure that you achieve the necessary grades, **(add a comma here as this is a list)** qualifications and experience needed to succeed in completing those objectives.

(New paragraph as the previous section was an introduction while this section details benefits of being in the Sixth Form) The Sixth Form should be more than just a finishing school for university and work. **(Add a full stop here as this is the end of one idea and the start of a new idea.)** In **(capital letter for the first word of a new sentence)** our Sixth Form, you will have the chance to: **(add a colon to introduce a list. The colon needs to come after the word 'to' since all the items in this list only make sense after the word 'to'.)** learn more study skills; develop personal qualities; **(add a semicolon since this is a complicated list. This should be obvious since all the other items are separated by semicolons.)** improve your time management; further extra-curricular interests; develop new sporting interests.

As a Sixth Former, **(add a comma after this introductory phrase where it would be natural to take a breath as a reader)** you are an integral part of the school. We expect you to take an active role in the school, **(add a comma before this additional piece of information where you would naturally make a** brief pause as a reader) which will make this one of the most enjoyable periods of your life. Your time in the Sixth Form will pass very quickly, **(add a comma here before the coordinating conjuction 'and')** and it's **(add an apostrophe here as this is a contraction)** important that you adjust to the demands of 16-19 education very quickly. You must remember that a key element of Sixth Form life is openness and honesty; if you are experiencing pastoral or academic difficulties causing you to be behind with deadlines, do not suffer in silence - come and talk to us. The school motto – "Together We Learn, Achieve and Succeed" **(close the speech marks at the end of the school motto.)** – is a good phrase to learn and remember while studying here.

Grammar (10 marks)

Task A – b, b, a

Task B – a, d, b, b

Task C – c, d, b

Task A

Dear Parent/Carer,

There is an exciting opportunity for your child to attend a residential trip to the beautiful and historic birthplace of Shakespeare, Stratford-Upon-Avon, from 7-9 December 2018. This trip will be run jointly between the English and Drama departments,

a) and will vastly enrich your childs' knowledge and skills in both subjects, whilst being great fun and providing them with lifelong memories. *(Incorrect position of the apostrophe.)*

b) **and will vastly enrich your child's knowledge and skills in both subjects, whilst being great fun and providing them with lifelong memories.**

c) vastly enriching your childs' knowledge and skills in both subjects, whilst being great fun and providing them with lifelong memories. *(Incorrect position of the apostrophe.)*

d) and will enrich your child's knowledge and skills vastly in both subjects, whilst being great fun and providing them with lifelong memories. *('Vastly enrich' sounds much better than 'enrich vastly'.)*

As your child will study a Shakespeare text as well as the Victorian classic novella, 'A Christmas Carol', for their English GCSE, we will be focusing on these areas to give your child the best head start we can,

a) whilst also provide them with unique opportunities far beyond the curriculum. *(The '-ing' form of the verb is grammatically correct after 'whilst' in the absence of a subject pronoun.)*

b) **whilst also providing them with unique opportunities far beyond the curriculum.**

c) whilst also providing them with opportunities far beyond the unique curriculum. *(It is the opportunities that are unique and not the curriculum.)*

d) whilst also providing unique opportunities for them far beyond the curriculum. *('Providing them with' is far more economical and concise than 'providing opportunities for them'.)*

This trip will be packed full with exciting activities and

a) **will minimise any disruption to the rest of your child's subjects as they will miss only one day of school.**

b) minimises any disruption to the rest of your child's subjects as they will miss only one day of school. *(Inconsistency in verb tense. The future tense is used in the question, but this answer option has switched to the present tense.)*

c) should minimise any disruption to the rest of your child's subjects as they will miss only one day of school. *(If I were writing a letter, I would try and be more positive and would use 'will' over 'should'.)*

d) minimises any disruption to the rest of your child's subjects as they are missing only one day of school. *(Inconsistency in verb tense. The future tense is used in the question, but this answer option has switched to the present tense.)*

Task B

At Wigan Academy, we strongly believe in the education of the whole child and having a broad and balanced curriculum that supports all learners.

a) **Pupils wishing to gain an understanding of the modern world can do so through Travel & Tourism.**

b) Pupils who wish to gain an understanding of the modern world can do so through Travel & Tourism. *(This sentence is fine, but 'pupils wishing to' is more economical and concise than 'pupils who wish to'.)*

c) Pupils that wish to gain an understanding of the modern world can do so through Travel & Tourism. *(You cannot use 'that' after people.)*

d) Pupils wish to gain an understanding of the modern world can do so through Travel & Tourism. *('Pupils wish to gain' simply doesn't make sense from a grammatical point of view in this sentence.)*

Our values-driven curriculum is enhanced further with an RE and PSHE curriculum that embraces the development of the whole child,

a) raises their awareness of all aspects of Spirituality, Social Justice, and Moral Conduct and supporting pupils to become well-rounded citizens ready to tackle the challenges of the modern world. *(The verb 'supporting' is grammatically incorrect in this sentence.)*

b) raises their awareness of all aspects of Spirituality, Social Justice, and Moral Conduct and supports pupils to become well-rounded citizens ready to tackle the challenges of the modern world. *(You could be forgiven for selecting this as a correct option as there is not much wrong with it, but 'd' is better. The use of 'raising' in 'd' is better as the '-ing' form of the verb is used to show that this is the consequence of the child having been developed.)*

c) raise their awareness of all aspects of Spirituality, Social Justice, and Moral Conduct and supporting pupils to become well-rounded citizens ready to tackle the challenges of the modern world. *(The verbs 'supporting' and 'raise' need to match. 'Raise' is definitely not correct as it would require a plural subject, and there isn't one.)*

d) **raising their awareness of all aspects of Spirituality, Social Justice, and Moral Conduct, and supports pupils to become well-rounded citizens ready to tackle the challenges of the modern world.**

Beyond the classroom pupils have many opportunities

a) to deepen their love of learning, supported when they need support, and to gain stretch and challenge when they wish to go above and beyond the standard curriculum. *(All the verb phrases have 'to' in front of 'the', with the exception of 'supported'.)*

b) **to deepen their love of learning, to be supported when they need support, and to gain stretch and challenge when they wish to go above and beyond the standard curriculum.**

c) to deepen their love of learning, to be supported when they need support, and gaining stretch and challenge when they wish to go above and beyond the standard curriculum. *(All the verb phrases have 'to' in front of 'the', with the exception of 'gaining'.)*

d) for deepening their love of learning, for being supported when they need support, and for gaining stretch and challenge when they wish to go above and beyond the standard curriculum. *(The repetition of 'for' sounds awkward. Better English would be to use 'to' after opportunities rather than 'for'.)*

Each child can expect to

a) be taught by a subject expert, who is continually challenging all learners to achieve there very best. *('There' is the incorrect spelling.)*

b) **be taught by a subject expert, who will be continually challenging all learners to achieve their very best.**

c) be taught by experts in the subject, who will be continually challenging all learners to achieve there very best. *('There' is the incorrect spelling. In addition, 'subject expert' reads better than 'experts in the subject'.)*

d) be taught by a subject expert, who will be continually challenging all learners to their best achievement. *('To their best achievement' is not good English. "To achieve their very best' is definitely preferable.)*

Task C

We are proud of our outstanding summer 2018 results, which build on the excellent results achieved in 2017 which placed the school in the top 5% nationally for student progress.

a) The outcome for both student progress and achievement evidence our distinctiveness and effectiveness as a Church of England School. *(There is no agreement between the singular subject 'the outcome' and the verb 'evidence'.)*

b) The outcomes for both student progress and achievement evidences our distinctiveness and effectiveness as a Church of England School. *(There is no agreement between the plural subject 'the outcomes' and the verb 'evidences'.)*

c) The outcomes for both student progress and achievement evidence our distinctiveness and effectiveness as a Church of England School.

d) The outcomes for student progress and achievement both evidence our distinctiveness and effectiveness as a Church of England School. *(The sequence 'both....and...' is correct English whereas 'and....both....' is not.)*

The Attainment 8 score

a) gives an indication of the raw grades that students would have achieved in the qualifications that they studied. *(The use of the past conditional 'would have' makes no sense in this sentence.)*

b) gives an indication of the raw grades that students had achieved in the qualifications that they studied. *(The use of the pluperfect tense 'had' makes no sense in this sentence.)*

c) gives an indication of the raw grades that students will have achieved in the qualifications that they studied. *(The use of the future perfect 'will have' makes no sense in this sentence.)*

d) **gives an indication of the raw grades that students have achieved in the qualifications that they studied.**

However, this value is very much dependant on the academic ability of the cohort of students which is indicated by the APS on entry.

a) An academic cohort of students would achieve high grades yielding a large attainment 8 score but have a poor progress score. *(The use of 'would' makes the intended meaning of this sentence extremely unclear.)*

b) **An academic cohort of students could achieve high grades yielding a large attainment 8 score but have a poor progress score.**

c) An academic cohort of students should achieve high grades yielding a large attainment 8 score but have a poor progress score. *(The use of 'should' in the same sentence with 'but have...' means the sentence does not make sense.)*

d) An academic cohort of students achieves high grades yielding a large attainment 8 score but have a poor progress score. *(The use of the word 'have' is grammatically incorrect. Even if it were correct, the sentence would still be confusing at best.)*

Reading comprehension answers (10 marks)

Task A

FIRST – 3

SECOND – 5

THIRD - 1

Task B

1, 4, 6, 9

Task C

1 – illegality

2 – irrationality

3 – procedural impropriety